Urdu Literature and Journalism

Critical Perspectives

Shafey Kidwai

Chairman, Department of Mass Communication
Aligarh Muslim University, Aligarh

FOUNDATION BOOKS

Bengaluru • Chennai • Delhi • Hyderabad • Kolkata • Mumbai • Pune • Thiruvananthapuram

FOUNDATION®
BOOKS

Foundation Books is an imprint of Cambridge University Press India Pvt. Ltd.

Cambridge House, 4381/4 Ansari Road, Daryaganj, New Delhi 110 002

www.cambridgeindia.org

First published 2014

Printed in India at Bhavish Graphics, Chennai

ISBN 978-93-82993-77-3 Paperback

For Shaista

Contents

Preface

Urdu, incorporating the heterogeneous aesthetic sensibilities, pluralistic perceptions, and different literary traditions which represent our age-old cultural and linguistic coalescence and shared social legacy, is certainly more than one of the languages listed in The Eight Schedule of our Constitution. Urdu, despite being derided by some quarters as a language of listless sophistication and mannerism, is essentially a creative accumulation of diverse cultural sentience including the emerging paradigm of subaltern discourse. It will not be an exaggeration to describe Urdu as a way of thinking and a style of life. It is what constitutes the much-admired mosaic of the cultural plurality of India.

Urdu always espouses the cause of unity of humankind, broadmindedness, fellow feeling and magnanimity by deploring the feigned sectarianism. No one can pass over the longstanding tradition of brotherly love unfailingly propagated by Urdu. Creative genius of its widely admired poets such as Meer, Ghalib, Firaq and Faiz was extremely instrumental in making the plural, democratic and liberal Indian society. It is nothing but sheer injustice to equate such an elegant language to a particular religion. Urdu stunningly exemplifies the essence of Indian culture, tolerance and forbearance. Urdu is yet to get its rightful place in its birthplace, and the perpetual neglect of the language hardly goes with the pluralistic culture of the country. Urdu literature always inspires awe, and a careful reading of Meer Taqi Meer, Ghalib, Iqbal, Prem Chand, Manto, Rajendra Singh Bedi, Qurratarul Ain Haider, Firaq Gorakhpuri, Makhdoom, Kaifi, Majrooh, Sardar Jafri, Shaheryar, Nida Fazli, Gulzar, Javed Akhtar and Salam Bin Razzaque, makes it clear that Urdu literature is far greater than dreamy-eyed adolescent experiences expressed in ornate style and sentimental imagery. The contemporary Urdu writers look beyond despair, angst, and anguish with hope and faith. They creatively explore the dynamics of cultural plurality, and the celebration of the emergence of empowered voices is at the centre of their creation. Not much has been written especially in English about how Urdu literature got itself disentangled from the bond of modernism and why narrative of alienation, isolation, persecution, dislocation and relocation no longer emerges as the dominant metaphor of the literature. This is what Shafey Kidwai, who is well-acquainted with the new trends of both eastern and western literary theories, has meticulously documented. His collection of essays containing the fruits of penetrating critical insights titled, *Urdu Literature and Journalism: Critical Perspectives*, weaves various strands of thoughts and stylistic variation to produce a richly-imagined kaleidoscopic portrait of contemporary Urdu literature and journalism. His book is a testimony to multitudes of crosscurrents sweeping across Urdu literature, and the main strength of the essays lies in their close scientific analysis of the text in the backdrop of perspective scaffoldings that keep the reader riveted. One can see a sustained interest in Urdu literature at a time when the number of Urdu-knowing people has continuously been dwindling. Shafey Kidwai's articles are aimed at providing a more precise understanding in intellectual terms about Urdu literature.

His essay, 'Post-Independence Urdu Short Story: The Indian Perspective', rightly points out that modern Urdu short story becomes a mask to mirror the paradoxical shadow lines of reality and fiction. Depiction of social reality has become lackluster, and Urdu short stories try to capture the emotional lay in a language, which is being constantly structured and deconstructed in a very Derridian sense.

The analysis of the stories is not confined to paraphrasing of themes, rather the author closely examines the text in the backdrop of story narratology and discourse analysis. Again, he rightly points out that post-modernism has gained currency in Urdu literature, and short stories renounce alienation and despair propagated by modernism. The stories are soothingly optimistic portraying the tension-fraught world that we live in. Prem Chand, Manto, Bedi, Ismat Chughtai, Qurratatul Ain Haider, Surendra Parkash, Salam Bin Razzaque, Syed Mohammad Ashraf and Tariq Chattari et cetera are discussed with acute sensitivity. Various strands of post-partition Urdu poetry are aptly explicated making it clear that Urdu poetry does not draw its sustenance from the woolly aesthetics and post-modern Urdu poetry is certainly more than verbal wizardry. Extensive deep reading and perceptive analysis provide much needed aid to uninitiated readers and it takes the reader out from the poet's insulated world.

Poetry always denotes creative subversion, and Shafey Kidwai, while analyzing the poems of Akhtarul Iman, Balraj Komal, Shaheryar, Salahuddin Pervez, Khalil Mamoon and Shaista Yusuf, lays bare the defiant gesture that poets make against numbing materialism and insensitivity.

A whole chapter is devoted to structuralism and post-structuralism in Urdu criticism; it turns attention to the epistemological and theoretical perspectives of literary theories that invariably surface even in the theory-avoidance-prone Urdu criticism. It is truly an intervention in the current discourse debate about reading of the text. He dispassionately examines the historical perspective as well as the emerging contours of modern literary theories and explains how structuralism and post-structuralism reveals what the author intends to conceal. He exposes many embarrassing contradictions of new criticism with remarkable ease. He looks at ways in which Urdu criticism lead the way towards a harmonious and acceptable literary canon.

The acute critical sensibility makes the author record what is coming, and it is fully reflected in the essay 'Jayant Parmar: The first voice of Dalit Poetry in Urdu'. He skillfully analyses different poems of Jayant to highlight the otherness of the debate on the nativity. Jayant's laconic poems examine the very notion of poetry from multicultural subjectivity. Here, one can see post-colonial disjunction of the self and the cherished ideals. With his discerning critical eye, Shafey Kidwai describes Jayant's creative outpouring as a discourse of the personal loss that hardly offers any clue to solve the question of the dislocated cultural space that encompasses the canvas of his poetry.

Two substantial essays 'Firaq as a Critic' and 'Literature, Culture and Social Consciousness: An Appraisal in Faiz's Prose Writings' bring together the diverse strands of critical acuity of our two widely-admired poets, Firaq Gorakhpuri and Faiz Ahmad Faiz. Here the author exclusively relies on direct quotes that produce starling perceptive approach of some well-known literary texts. In their prose writings, both Firaq and Faiz seem incisive, and shocking without being too harsh, and their interpretation of the text incorporates with its texture a discourse on the very nature of depiction of reality. The prose betrays their awakening on all fronts: literary theory, cultural, social and political.

Ghalib has an epic sweep and his poetry continues to be a revealing portrait of our muddled and chaotic present. He remains at the centre of critical gaze, and it is daunting for anyone to make a detailed appraisal of what has been written on Ghalib. Many scholars and critics presented an insightful view of the richness of Persio-Arabic and Indian poetical tradition that aptly manifested in Ghalib's poetry, but many books on Ghalib are deathly listless and the essay 'Ghalib Criticism: An overview', looks at the interpretation offered by some critics, reviewing the whole corpus of Ghalib criticism with a flourish.

Tagore's creative genius has left an indelible mark on the collective psyche of Indian writers, and Urdu is no exception. It is interesting to note that Munshi Prem Chand discussed Tagore's work quite often in his articles and letters much before the Nobel Prize was conferred upon Tagore. The author has taken pains in tracing the influence of Tagore on Urdu literature.

Shafey Kidwai has also written extensively on the history of vernacular journalism with remarkable thoroughness, which is clearly manifested in the articles that form the second section of the book. The author revealed that Sir Syed did work for a Persian newspaper, a fact which is not well-known. He supplemented what has been left out by Hayat-e-Javed.

Dispassionate textual analysis aiming at a more incise understanding is the common strand that runs through all articles. Shafey Kidwai is alive to new theoretical paradigm and literary canon. His prose does avoid unnecessary explication, and lucidity of expression lends readability to the appealing nature of the articles. Bereft of linguistic glitches and hackneyed literary terms, his critical analysis is richly imagined and brilliantly executed. The collection certainly brightens up new dimensions of the ongoing debate about how to study literature.

Gopi Chand Narang
Former President
Sahitya Akademi
New Delhi

Introduction

Scarcely does a language endure as much agony in its own homeland as Urdu, and that too in the hands of those who describe it as the controlling metaphor of their distinct cultural identity as the majority of its native speakers, mostly living in north India, no longer use it as a means of communication, and the new generation is hardly even aware of its script. Still bearing the brunt of the Partition, Urdu finds it extremely difficult to preserve its script due to a continual fall in its use. However, notwithstanding the apparent decline, the language is still spoken by more than 60 million people (2001 census) in India and the literature in Urdu by distinguished poets and fiction writers like Meer, Ghalib, Iqbal, Premchand, Manto, Bedi, Firaq, Faiz, Nasir Kazmi, Ahmad Faraz, Intizar Hussain, and Shaheryar draws immense adulation from all quarters.

Urdu has won a fair share of admirers for its ingrained quality of bringing different cultural sensibilities together as well as detractors for allegedly championing the cause of the Partition. In this backdrop, one has to study Urdu literature, and the articles included in this book are braced for understanding the dynamics of the power of cultural paradox that is evidently manifested in the case of Urdu. What kind of cultural and ethnic identity is being fostered by Urdu literature? Who are the prominent authors of the post-Partition Urdu literature? These questions are delineated in these articles that revolve around Urdu writers in India. This book, an assortment of twelve essays, is an attempt to analyze Urdu's inherent prowess of strengthening liberal values, pluralism and ingesting new literary trends, ideological positions and current socio-political discourses. Here, a sustained effort is made to initiate and develop an informed debate on those aspects of contemporary Urdu literature that have not been discussed thoroughly. These essays try to engage those ideological positions that view literature as an entity which cling to social and cultural practices. It goes without saying that literature is firmly grounded in social and cultural milieu of a particular country but one must realize that new literary insights, theories, hermeneutics, structuralism and post-structuralism are in no way confined to the specific geographical boundaries.

The essays are written with a diverse spectrum of readers in mind. They deal with a distinct intellectual tradition that continues to invigorate Urdu literature. Urdu journalism, since its inception (Jam-e-Jahan Numa, 1822, Calcutta), has been perceived as a body of polemical, atonal and sentimental outpouring. But a careful and dispassionate perusal of the writings of some prominent Urdu journalists does not endorse this widely-held view. Conversely, their writings prove that Urdu journalism played a pivotal role in popularizing liberal values, national consciousness and modern education in the Moulvi-oppressed society of the nineteenth century India, but a section of Urdu periodical still tries to perpetuate a sense of being victimised among its gullible readers, and they hardly provide anything beyond rhetorical crutches.

The twelve articles, written over the past several years, are updated and drawn together in a collection. They deal with Urdu literature and Urdu journalism and try to equip the reader with a fair understanding of both. The book aims to acquaint readers with new theoretical discourses artistically manifested in contemporary Urdu short story, poetry and criticism. It intends to cater to the needs of academics interested in the development of Urdu literature as well as of those who read Urdu poetry and fiction for aesthetic pleasure. A marked emphasis on readability, objective analysis of the text and the inclusion of different opinions and perspectives runs through the collection. The articles, diverse in theme and import, have an intense analytical approach, and appraisal of the text is usually done with clarity of thought and expression.

The first section of this book comprises eight essays pertaining to various genres of Urdu literature. The first chapter titled, 'Post-Independence Urdu short story: The Indian perspective' attempts to identify emerging trends in terms of ideological concerns and fast-changing narrative strategy employed by the modern short story writers. Modern Urdu short story, inheriting a lot from Premchand and Manto, embraces new modes of storytelling with abundant enthusiasm. Naiyar Masood, Tariq Chaṭtari, Syed Mohammad Ashraf and Khalid Javed used the work of their predecessors as an ongoing process of discovery. For them, literary landmark is not a prison but a creative resource. The author tries to show what short story inherits and how it recreates the past. Frequent inclusion of non-fiction elements coupled with narrative fluency has become the most distinct feature of the contemporary short story, and it betrays the author's growing interest as a historian as well as a storyteller. A close study of the texts of Paigham Afaqi, Ghaznafar, Shaukat Hayat, Siddiq Alam, Tarranum Riyaz and Baig Ehsas reveal how effectively they articulate mundane and ephemeral issues with artistic prowess. Their stories also document their keen – almost intuitive – understanding of the challenges of the world around them. They are sympathetic to their characters but don't gloss over their inherent flaws and shortcomings. They do not try to mould the actions and ideas of the characters into a unified point of view. Though the post-modern short story is gaining currency rapidly, it is often being pilloried by Marxist and modernist mindset.

Despite its inclination to use evocative idioms and paradox judiciously, post-Partition Urdu poetry no longer restricts itself to providing its readers with just aesthetic pleasure. It continuously strives for their minds. It does not overwhelm the reader with clichés but acquaints them with various layers of human drama of suspicion, hostility and emotional betrayal. It is still driven by rage and scorn but Urdu poets like Firaq Gorakhpuri, Akhtar ul Iman and Shaheryar make self-denial an exhilarating reading experience without indicating even a smattering of remorse. The second chapter of this book deals with many other aspects of modern Urdu poetry.

How does articulation of one's anguish give readers an opportunity to rediscover themselves? How does oblivion drawing heavily from the tumult of memory, confusion, emotion and anxiety become synonymous with the cessation of all awareness? Such questions have also been dealt with in this chapter.

The third chapter traces the overt, indirect and even diffused influence of new theoretical frameworks and literary trends on Urdu criticism with a study of the critical essays of prominent Urdu critics. It tries to unravel the contours of the contemporary Urdu criticism and argues that although new critical insights sometimes surface in the form of applied criticism, there is a definite scarcity of insightful readings of well-known texts. Urdu criticism is never found wanting in incorporating newly-arrived ideas as it used them to brighten up the otherwise dour writings.

The fourth chapter makes it clear that Jayant Parmar's poetry denotes an engaging departure from cliché-ridden idiom of Urdu poetry as the poet unravels various layers of a schism that runs through the lives of the marginalized. The first dalit poet of Urdu, Jayant does not ruminate obsessively over the past as his life is driven by disdain and exclusion, and he refuses to attribute anything gratifying to his immediate past.

Firaq Gorakhpuri's critical insight has come in for a detailed discussion in the fifth chapter. The close study of Firaq's prose acquaints the reader with his magnificent sweep, and one finds it eminently readable. He analyzes the text with empathy, grace and occasionally with remarkable astuteness and is further embellished by gentle humour and deep insights.

Ghalib's awe-inspiring creativity is invested with tremendous potentiality of unleashing cerebral riffs, and it continues to capture the attention of scholars and critics. The sixth chapter presents an overview of all the perspectives in Ghalib criticism. A deliberate attempt is made to achieve a critical space that paves the way for comparing different critical approaches adopted by many critics to analyze Ghalib's poetry.

The seventh chapter focuses on Faiz's prose writings and discusses his concept of literature out of a wider analysis of his articles pertaining to culture, traditions, literary convictions, and social practice. The articles make it clear that Faiz's prose writing may serve as a useful guide both on theoretical and practical counts for would-be-authors. His prose is free from rigorous discipline required in criticism, but it betrays his meticulous analytical ability and graceful ease at analyzing the different semantic layers of the text.

Rabindranath Tagore's unprecedented capacity of capturing all the complexities of human existence in his works continues to stimulate creative writers of different languages spoken across the country, and Urdu is no exception. Chapter eight traces the influence of Tagore on Urdu literature and makes it clear that Tagore's creative trove is still considered as an inexhaustible source of wisdom and inspiration.

The second section of this book, comprising four articles, deals with Urdu journalism in pre- and post-Partition India.

Sir Syed is widely known as the founder of the Aligarh Muslim University, but people hardly acknowledge his pivotal role for spreading education among Muslims with the help of two periodicals. Sir Syed's contribution to journalism is still not well-documented. The ninth chapter presents a detailed account of Sir Syed's journalistic writings. In his formative years, he found journalism the most effective medium of persuading Muslims to come out of their medieval grooves. He wrote with brutal objectivity. It exacted a price not many were willing to pay, and so his writing was criticized.

Not recognized widely, Urdu has many firsts to its credit. The first book on the art of journalism in any Indian language was published in Urdu. The book, published in 1938, is discussed in the tenth chapter.

Widely-circulated Urdu periodicals of the early nineeth century were instrumental in arousing public sentiment against the alien rulers. They also extended wholehearted support to the First War of Independence. Moulvi Mohammad Baqar, editor of *Delhi Urdu Akhbar*, was the first Indian journalist who laid his life for the country. This aside, the contribution of Urdu journalists to the First War of Independence is deliberated in the eleventh chapter.

The last chapter places great emphasis on analyzing the journalistic writings of Maulana Abul Kalam Azad from a professional point of view. Maulana Azad used journalism as the most intimate medium of initiating a debate on all aspects of life, and his deep concern for mitigating the sufferings of Indians is frequently reflected in his writings. His periodicals unfailingly manifest his alert and unprejudiced point of view and his abiding concerns for his fellow countrymen.

The essays on Urdu newspaper prove that Urdu journalism is certainly more than, 'Protest journalism', a term that has been widely – though erroneously – used for Urdu periodicals. It is the first collection of my articles that appeared in journals.

I would like to express my gratitude to a number of my relatives, scholars, and friends whose suggestions have helped along the way. I am greatly indebted to Professor Gopi Chand Narang, eminent scholar, theorist, critic and former president of National Academy of letters, for his constant encouragement and guidance. I am thankful to my parents late Habib Ahad Kidwai and late Humaira Khatoon, uncle late Hakim Abdul Qavi (Editor, *Sidq Jadeed*, Lucknow) and my brother-in-law Abdul Rehman Salman Alvi who initiated me into literature and journalism. I am also grateful to my father-in-law Rashid Faridi, mother-in-law Qamar Faridi, brothers Abdul Rafay Kidwai, Abdul Nafay Kidwai, Abdul Ali Kidwai, brothers-in-law Fazeel and Rishad Faridi, Shimail and Bushra Faridi who inspired me to write.

Above everyone else, I would like to express my heartfelt gratitude to my wife Shaista Faridi for her constant support. I am also thankful to her and my sons Sharif and Shaghil for not being impatient as I usually have to spend long hours away from them.

I owe an enormous gratitude to Mr Ziya us Salam, an accomplished literary critic and reviewer for being a constant source of encouragement.

Thanks are due to my friends Nasir Abbas Naiyer, Syed Asim Ali, Shoeb Nizam, Shikoh Mohsin Mirza, Mohsin Khan and Nadeem Ashraf. I am also thankful to Saad Bin Zia, Guest Faculty, Department of Mass Communication, Shamimuzzaman, Assistant Public Relations officer, Mohammad Anas, Research Scholar, Department of Mass Communication, and Sagheer Ahmad, Administrative Assistant, Department of Mass Communication, for their invaluable assistance.

Finally, I would like to thank Cambridge University Press India Pvt. Ltd. for taking up the project for publication and providing vital inputs that enabled me to keep a safe distance from cliché and euphemism. Without their perceptive suggestions this book would not have materialized.

Shafey Kidwai

Acknowledgements

The author and publishers of this book are grateful to the following for permission to reprint articles which were originally published by them:

Sanchar Shri, research journal of Department of Mass Communication, Lucknow University, for permission to reprint 'Abul Kalam Azad's Journalistic Conquests', originally published as 'Maulana Azad's Journalistic Endeavours'.

Prof Shahabuddin Iraqi, Editor of Sir Syed Vision and Mission Volume, for permission to reproduce 'Early Journalistic Endeavours of Sir Syed Ahmad Khan', originally published as 'Early Journalistic Endeavours of Sir Syed'

Sahitya Akademi for permission to reproduce the articles 'Post-Independence Urdu Short Story', drawn from 'Urdu Literature: A Survey' and 'Post-Partition Urdu Poetry', originally published as 'Post-Independence Urdu Poetry' published in *Indian Literature* in the issues of November–December 1995 and September–October 2001 respectively.

1. Post-Independence Urdu Short Story

The Indian Perspective

Since the short story, unlike poetry, frequently unfolds the humdrum of daily domesticity, it has been perceived as a body of writing that hardly transcends the common place experiences of life. Short story, by its very nature, zeroes in on a reality that is not only multidimensional and far more pernicious but also has an unpredictable element that shapes our day-to-day life. In line with its above-mentioned defining theme, the short story also turns our attention to some eternal verities that constitute the mainstay of human existence.

It tries to highlight the wholeness and richness of an experience in its entirety by presenting things in diverse perspectives. Set in both urban and rural milieu, stories unfailingly form a template for coming to terms with external reality, and the trials and tribulations of the characters pave the way for self-discovery. The characters unfold themselves in dribs and drabs and one can also come across a plethora of protagonists whose actions are both self-revelatory and self-concealing. They show tacit support for lifelong rectitude.

Urdu short story, right from the beginning, reflected its immense zest in focussing on 'shimmerness of life', a phrase frequently used by D. H. Lawrence. Pandit Ratan Nath Sarshar, Nazeer Ahmad and Mirza Hadi Ruswa laid the foundation of Urdu fiction and they depicted the multifaceted reality of life with rare dexterity. Social reform was the central theme of the early short stories and growing inclination toward external reality gave it a distinct form and it broke away from popular fables and tales.

Premchand's stress on the mores of rural life gradually took the Urdu short story into the realm of realism. Premchand's first short story 'Anmol Ratan' appeared in 1907. In this story, he blended idealism and social realism with multiple focalisations through different characters while the storyline presented a more vivid and sustained vision of reality. His narrative centred on the despicable violence unleashed upon the toiling farmers in British India.

With him, native sensibility or an abiding concern for self-respect became a distinctive feature of Urdu fiction. Premchand's creative genius coupled with his constant insistence on a realist narrative also resulted in a quest for an expression of the complex interplay of the inner reality and the outer world.
Analyzing Premchand's short stories, David Rubin points out:

> By the example of his work he transformed fiction in these languages (Urdu and Hindi) from rambling romantic chronicles or didactic tales to a high level of realistic narrative comparable to naturalistic European fiction.
>
> (1988: 3)

Sadat Hasan Manto had a unique gift of turning the familiar modes of storytelling and thematic mannerism upside down. He was the first fiction writer in any Indian language who made it a point to record almost every pulse of human existence that is downright despicable and nugatory. He was intrigued and fascinated by utilitarianism, slave morality and the trendy ideologies of his time.

His stories betray a distinct narrative strategy that borders on transgression. His world is not devoid of moral values, but it quite visibly inches toward anarchy where outlandishness becomes an ideal retreat. Manto's characters are unpredictable. They vividly reveal the abstruseness and intricacies of the human psyche. The coalescence of unpremeditated events intensifies dramatic fervour and psychological density.

Far from treading on the path of realist and romantic writers, Manto endeavours to repudiate the mannerism and feigned morality practised by both the upper and middle classes. The imperceptible quivering of selfishness found in human nature also fires his imagination and he amuses himself with these individual failings.

Manto's penetrating irony has placed him at the acme of realism that is both manifold and variegated. His stories essentially mock sentimentalism in literature and he unwittingly assumes the role of a burlesque critic. Manto is primarily concerned with the common man who has no idealised image of himself. He struggles to live the ordinariness of life in a hassle-free manner.

Manto's much-acclaimed stories 'Toba Tek Singh', 'Khol Do'. 'Naya Qanoon', 'Babu Gopi Nath' and some other stories supply major clues to his rancour about the partition and the subsequent macabre dance of death and destruction. His creative world does not present a dull summary of the unprecedented violence recorded on the pages of history but concentrates on how men behave in a completely altered social context and how does fiendishness gain currency all around.

Prostitutes appear in Manto's stories quite often, but their tales are completely devoid of vicarious thrills. The frequent reference to flesh trade hardly indicates any voyeurism and Manto makes prostitutes objects of a single pristine focus. Promiscuity and deceit also irritate the author, but he is not swayed by anger and portrays even the unpleasant characters with rare objectivity. His narration exudes a deep sense of sympathy.

The readers are encouraged to travel into the most intricate and enigmatic regions of the characters' natures and ego. The author hatches an inconclusive and non-discursive narrative paradigm and his narration is heightened by the use of concise, pithy phrases and ironic posing. Sometimes trenchant comments are communicated in a comical and playful manner. His stories 'Phundney', 'Sarak Ke Kinare', 'Babu Gopinath' and the like bear an eloquent testimony to the fact. A number of stories including 'Sarak Ke Kinare' and 'Bu' are good examples of ecriture feminine. He sometimes employs pseudo logical vocabulary to invest dialogues with ironic posing.

Taking cue from Bakhtin, Gopichand Narang, an eminent Urdu critic, describes Manto's stories as dialogic or polyphonic as many voices indicating divergent point of view emerge simultaneously and the author makes no attempt to reconcile all the contradictions inherent in that situation.

Turning attention to Manto's famous character Babu Gopinath, Narang conclusively argues:

> Manto's characters are the creation of the author but they are not necessarily fastened together with the author's point of view. Babu Gopinath is a very different and interesting character. It is interesting to note that here the author is present all through and his pith comments turn the end into an ironical penitence. Without the fear of contradiction, he is the best example of polyphony in Urdu short story.
>
> (2009: 84)

Another prominent Urdu fiction writer was Rajendra Singh Bedi who wrote extensively after Independence. His subject matter was predominantly Indian and he responded aesthetically to some of the radical structural changes occurring in the country. Bedi's preoccupation with social narrative did not deter him from alluding to the polarity of life. At the same time, he expressed human suffering in his stories without any rhetorical rush.

In his creative world, the traditional epistemological premises of cause and effect centric narratives do not break into a cascade of thought. Bedi meticulously makes use of myths, allegory, archetypes, legends and folk tales, but his focus remains on reinterpretation, subversion and the creation of new myths. His writing unfailingly presents a situation shaped by the ambivalent attitude of the contemporary society. The indelible impression his stories leave is that of despair and bewilderment. His short stories basically deal with the ephemeral but stark realities of life; it is worth mentioning that his narration is bereft of jargon, pretension and inane gaudiness.

Bedi's characters exude mixed reaction towards the present Indian domestic life. His stories revolve around women who relentlessly toil for the betterment of the family, but their painstaking efforts, ameliorative in nature, hardly get recognised. The unsung heroine, whether a beloved, a sister, a wife or a mother, inspires Bedi, who candidly portrays the traditional Indian women in the altered and ever-changing social context.

The portrayal of Indian womanhood prompts Professor Gopi Chand Narang to point out:

> Bedi does not idealize woman but the suffering, enduring and tolerating nature of his character imparts to them a touch of sanctity, a breath of greatness. The woman in Bedi's stories, whether a beloved, wife or mother, is the suffering soul of creation, the all pervasive spirit, the mother of the whole universe.
>
> (2009: 92)

Sometimes Bedi's narration draws its sustenance from mawkishness that closely borders on kitsch. 'Methun', 'Garhan', 'Lajvanti' and 'Apne Dukh Mujhe De Do' present a graphic account of individual failings and triumphs. In these stories, the omniscient or the occasionally intrusive narrator frequently makes disparaging comments while the embedding sequences of the events unfurl the story that leaves the reader delightfully bewildered.

Bedi deliberately creates new myths on the pattern of ancient myths and the primal images.

> Narang in his seminal essay 'Rajendra Singh Bedi's Art: Metaphorical and Mythical Roots' analyzed his famous story 'Garhan' and asserted that Bedi blended a myth into a plot so as to transpose them into one another. In this story, the lunar eclipse and the earthly phenomenon running parallel to it conjures up a multisensory analogy. The heroine's fate too is under eclipse.
>
> (2009: 95)

Bedi has used myths with such telling effects so as to invest the story with a down-to-earth reality. The mythical characters exploring nostalgic and wistful experiences tell many stories. Myth is a semantic structure that provides conceptual and narrative support for a social world. Bedi uses pidgin language and discursive mode of narration in almost all of his stories. Not only does it reveal his lexical exuberance but makes him the most outstanding contemporary fiction writer as well.

The subtlest and most significant thoughts of philosophers, psychologists, linguists and anthropologists become an integral part of the fictional discourse of Qurratul Ain Haider. Far from presenting a listless paraphrasing of an idea, Qurratul Ain Haider explicates the sensuous, emotional and intellectual awareness of life. She opens new doors in Urdu fiction by discerningly applying the stream of consciousness and cinematic techniques of montage and flash back with a view to unsettling both the traditional mode of story telling and time sequence. With her extra ordinarily quick eye, she grasps various patterns of things seen and of things thought about. The deep anxiety about the saptiocultural identity unfailingly conveys the longing and near despair of the writer who is seemingly piqued at all pervading decline. She is completely lost to realize that universal truths have ceased to exist.

The ambivalence of modern life impels her to take refuge in the past which always enlivens her. Her writings centre on a decaying culture with a deep melancholic sense of dislocation. In her epoch-making novel *Aag Ka Dariya,* the cultural chronicle of the past and the dramatic conflict of socio-cultural space is presented with imagist perception, but there is no trace of lyrical rush and romantic outpouring of the experience.

Qurratul Ain Haider's deep concern with 'things that are lost' results in seeking refuge in skeptic questioning of the existentialist tradition in her fiction. *Aag Ka Dariya, Akhire-Shab Ke Hamsafar, Gardish-e-Rang-e-Chaman, Chandni Begum* and scores of short stories show her penchant for incorporating many diverse ideas without dishing out any valid creative reason.

The attempt to present a rejig of widely-held notions and human predicament results in a concentration on a complex mélange that is unerringly fixed. The threat of an indissoluble uniformity or Metanarrative prompts her to relocate the process of 'compression of space and time'. The past interspersed with the free flow of cross -cultural streams enkindles her imagination and she constructs the social saga of the fading culture of the upper class Muslims of North India.

Her themes, drawn from the nostalgic and wistful experience, betray her knack for creating a non-negotiable inner code. Her trail-blazing story 'Housing Society' portrays the partition in allegorical terms and time becomes a living embodiment of anguish. Dialogue, action, situation and physical mannerism, all reveal a strong sense of dejection.

Her other stories 'Roshni Ki Raftar', 'Nazzara Darmiyan Hain', 'Malfoozate Haji Gul Baba Bekatashi', and 'Agle Janam Mujhe Bitya Na Keejyu' unfailingly manifest a strong sense of new historicity and polarization of sensitivity. Qurratul Ain Haider catches the bull of realism by its horn in her relatively less acclaimed novel *Akhire Shab Ke Humsafar* in which she turns attention to human predicament. The protagonist Rehan Da, once a firebrand revolutionary, compromises with the reactionary forces and even joins the forces of counter revolution.

Ismat Chughtai's short story, 'Lihaf' opened new horizons of female consciousness upon the Urdu reader. The repressed female psyche and its subsequent demur at the denial of self-expression and self-assertion finds vivid description in this story that centers on non-conformist and atypical relationships. The story tears apart the sanctioned image of women, and in her creative world, one finds that the woman is no longer a goddess of chastity and has no visible traces of the supposed feminine identity.

Chugtai unleashes biting sarcasm on feigned and pharisaical righteousness. The plot or storyline in her short stories becomes subservient to her creative usage of language that does more than conveying the surface meaning or apparent reality. Her surprising images mirroring the most familiar material carry the reader to an underlying wealth of meaning. Sukrita Paul rightly observes that Ismat Chughtai's use of unique idioms and striking metaphors has received a lot of acclaim in Urdu.

The tales of courtesans and prostitutes are often narrated in Ismat's work. An excerpt from her famous short story 'Paisha' will prove the point:

> I was aware that she was a courtesan. That dyed red hair, those tight art fits and the crowd of men all the time. Music, dance, shrill and heavy laughter. These made me reel in my room without any reason. We women could defeat many a heavy weight, but an encounter with a courtesan and there goes all our feminity. This is the main reason that a mother while singing a lullaby to her child always emphasizes that a courtesan is a serpent, dragon and heaven knows what else.
>
> And this childhood abhorrence of the courtesan seems to have entered my blood stream. Let a thousand women cross my path I would not care, but the smell of a courtesan would make me alert like a targeted deer. I remembered that I happened to smell them first in my childhood. At Bahraich, at the sacred tomb of Sayyed Mian, every Thursday there used to be a gathering of the courtesans from all over the place. On those auspicious days pious and noble souls would also throng the tomb in larger than usual number.
>
> I do not know why one day a rather veteran courtesan picked me up in her arms. On her silken slippery dress and that peculiar aroma from her breast. I immediately climbed down from her arms.
>
> That day every one teased me at home that a prostitute had touched me. I felt such deep resentment that I kept on crying for a long time. Then one day an aunt of mine visited us. She kissed me and there it was, the same slippery dress and aromatic breast. I do not know why but I escaped from there.
>
> (*Indian Literature*, Issue No. 170, November-December, 1995: 62)

It is nothing but a full-throated cry against the oppression and societal abuse that is both timeless and widespread. Chugtai's short stories constantly strain against the peripheries imposed by the decadent society.

Kirshan Chander's stories, barring some exceptions, focus on social realism and touch upon the basic chord of human sensibility. 'Kalu Bhangi', 'Ann Data', 'Ghalicha', 'Mahalakshmi Ka Pul' 'Murda Samandar' et cetera conjure up an entire universe of pulsating emotions, and they also portray varied layers of life with conflicting characters and differing points of view. One can see different patterns of temporal experiences in these stories.

The textual presentation of events parodies the apparent intellectual experiences that closely resemble the half-interpreted predictions. Some of his stories betray his strong inclination towards the socialist system and he frequently uses highly euphuistic language.

In line with the tradition of Premchand, Hayatullah Ansari's fiction, especially his copious novel *Lahoo Ke Phool,* which runs into five volumes, set in a rural milieu, highlights socio-politically significant events of his time. His widely acclaimed short stories such as 'Shuker Guzar Ankhen', 'Akhri Koshish' and 'Bhare Bazar Mein' are written in the realist tradition but are rich in allegorical portrayal. They are structured to highlight the incorruptible values of truth. The never ending conflict between human destiny and day-to-day reality and the subsequent sufferings and agony is the binding theme of the short stories. A matter-of-fact style of narration is the hallmark of his realist fiction which sometimes borders on journalistic presentation.

The element of lamentation is quite evidently absent in the short stories of Jeelani Bano, that turn the spotlight on the much talked about exploitation of women who have been most unjustly and most arbitrarily denied their rightful claims to dignity. She creates a multi-faceted portrayal of the ethical paradigm of domestic life where the opposite acts of compassion and savagery are being performed by the same person. Surprisingly, it is the female protagonist who surfaces in a plethora of stories including 'Qable Marg' and 'Bahar ka Akhri Gulab'.

Jeelani Bano's latest collection of short stories, *Rasta Band Hai* (2010) carries twenty two character-oriented stories. The characters strive to wean their minds away from post-romantic obsession and they speak of their thwarted and unfulfilled desires and their anger that stayed repressed. Insensitivity and apathy of the state seem to be the most mundane and even prosaic topics, but the author has an amazing ability to transform these into an engaging narrative and her famous story 'Rasta Band Hai' is intrinsically attached to this truth. In the story, traffic is not allowed to ply as the chief minister intends to visit an area; the motorcade of the minister disappears and the political deadlock continues. Sagheer Afrahim rightly points out that the story ends without the arrival of the leader (2011).

Balwant Singh's stories reveal a new ground of regional writing and his characters depict all the earthly qualities of Punjab and its multi-layered and awe-inspiring cultural specifications, but his characters are invariably phallocentric. 'Jagga', 'Gobindi', 'Kathan' 'Dagariya', 'Granthi', 'Pahla Pather', 'Punjab Ka Albela' and 'Deemak' reflect his deep understanding of the cultural ethos of Punjab and its boisterous life style.

Professor Gopichand Narang, in his perceptive analysis of Balwant Singh's stories, writes:

> Some of Balwant Singh's stories go beyond the surface of sexual monotony leading boredom and dullness in life but 'Kathan Dagariya' is different. It delves deep into the libidinous drive and reveals several layers of meaning. Apparently it may seem that the man is the active agent and the woman is the passive receiver. The listless and uniform routine of every day life which dulls a man's emotion is not only man's problem but the problem of the woman too. The phallocentric culture of course regards man as the only active agent while in fact woman is an equal partner.
>
> It is not necessary that Balwant Singh wrote the story with the woman as the pivot. He just constructed a lively narrative through his artistic imagination. However, a basic question is touched, either through conscious design or otherwise. 'Kathan Dagariya' (Difficult Pathway) is the kind of story that may lend itself to deeper readings. In my opinion, it can subvert the expectation of the reader and go against conventional meaning. It is a story of an unpleasant truth and not of an idealised romance or some other story.
>
> Like 'Granthi' or 'Soorma Singh', 'Kathan Dagariya' is also a very well-constructed story where there is not a single word that is superfluous and the narration flows with extraordinary fluency.
>
> (1996)

Qazi Abdus Sattar's fiction, including his widely acknowledged short story 'Peetal Ka Ghanta' and novels *Shab Gazeeda* and *Badal* draw liberally from wistful experiences. The heart-rending and appalling but unavoidable disintegration of the noblesse provokes him to take a dig at the neo-rich class.

His other novels *Dara Sikoh, Ghalib* and *Khalid Bin Waleed* delve into ideas of historicity and cultural identity but frequent use of ostentatious language makes his writing atonal and sentimental. He hardly goes beyond heaping praise on the past and the past is not the one that is real but the one which the author conceives in his mind.

The new short story, committed to modern sensibility and the Kafkaesque tradition, made its appearance in Urdu, in the mid sixties. It owes much to Manto, Hasan Askari, Qurratul Ain Haider, Surendra Prakash and Balraj Mainra who changed the course of the modern short story as they abandoned realist narrative propagated by the progressive writers and started reflecting on a more complex notion of reality. Their stories showed a definite deviation from the realist form of narrative, and Joyce, Sartre, Camus and Kafka became the new sources of creative afflatus.

S.R. Farooqui, an eminent Urdu critic, is fully aware that often greater gains are accrued by reexamining the epistemological and theoretical framework of a popular genre of literature. His much talked about book on the contemporary Urdu short story, *Afsane ki Himayat mein*, puts a question mark on the existence of short story, one of the most admired genres of Urdu literature. For him, the modern short story goes beyond praising 'Kafan' and 'Phundane'. The book adroitly portrays incorrigible fallacies inherent in the very structure of short story. The book comprises eighteen short but equally forceful articles and is premised on the theoretical assumption that the short story is nowhere near to poetry as far as intricacy and elegance is concerned.The articles consistently try to convince the readers that the short story is universally inferior, second rate and a shoddy genre of literature, and for Farooqui, it occupies the position of the youngest son in the family, whose existence remains inconsequential.

> The biggest flaw of short story is its narrative disposition that can never be transmuted. It is not possible to reject narrative time and

> again. Dialogue and characters can be rejected and even abjuration of the plot makes the traces of narrative visible. One can upset the time sequence but one can not nullify time in short story. Short story is essentially fixed in a time frame; it is not possible to indicate that events do not take place in short story; hence radical changes are not possible here. By dissembling the plot one can upset the time sequence. It is the dead end. The first rate genre remains alert to perpetual changes. This is the limitation of the short story: it has no room for new experiments.
>
> (Farooqui, 2004)

Describing 'Kafan' as the best example of black humour, Farooqui says that Premchand's famous story breaks a new ground in Urdu. For him, had the author lived longer, he would have created many more characters resembling those of Madhav and Gheesu. The success of these characters lies in the fact that we hate and sympathise with them simultaneously. Premchand misses no opportunity in being judgmental, and here, he hurriedly passes judgment on the society but the author keeps his judgment reserved about Madhav and Gheesu or he leaves it up to us.

The issue of the plot, the problem of the story line in the short story, conflict of narration and character in the short story and some aspects of narrative are much talked about in his articles.

Farooqui's intent on looking down upon the short story unfailingly laid bare the outlook of a critic who firmly believes in the preferential order of various genres of literature.

His polemical dismissal of the short story met with equally hostile reactions. Waris Alvi and a number of fiction writers have powerfully refuted the argument that the short story cannot vie with poetry, as it hardly unfolds the intricate emotional and psychological fabric of man and also, stories do not reveal an intellectual spontaneity. Time frame and portrayal of events invest the story with new artistic coherence. Abid Suhail, a renowned short story writer, dispassionately tore apart all his arguments in his book, *Fiction Tanqeed Chand Bunyadi Mobahis.*

Farooqui's assertions managed to unsettle quite a few but he remained unfazed. This is not to deny that his book shows the way to negotiate with the uncharted path of narratology but at times his writings become dreary and preachy.

Balraj Mainra's stories, by their very nature, pull mimetic realism apart and his stories 'Machis' and 'Composition Series' explore the new configuration of the complexity of human relationship.

From the remains of realist short stories, Surendra Prakash fashioned a self-referential narrative that is braced for capturing the multi-faceted aspect of reality and the myriad impressions of it. With his writing, the traditional mode of storytelling that centres on a sequential plot, went astray. Even his apparently realist narrative is a perfect example of the narrative of dislocation and the last few lines of his famous short story 'Shadow Lines' bear testimony to the fact:

> When we reached Lucknow my own relatives and the relatives of Haji Saheb and Jahandida Hussain converged on my house. After the union some became sorrowful while others, willy-nilly, burst into tears. There were some who began to whisper among themselves.
>
> The following day Ayyub Bhai took the kèy from his wife and opened the room where his father had kept some of his belongings. He went in along with other members of his family and children. Some moments later we heard them crying. We peeped in to see what the matter was. There were old books, photographs and dresses spread before them. A big portrait was lying on one side. It was Wajid Ali Shah in Kathak mudra. After weeping copiously for sometime they came out.
>
> Their eyes were still moist. They did not close the room. The widow of Yaqub said, "Inder Bhai, this room needs tidying up". "Sure Bhabi Saheba, it'll be done immediately", responded my wife.
>
> Next day they went to the tomb of Hazart Bibi and visited all the old places and 'Imambaras' of Lucknow. They read 'Fateha' at each place. The cycle of prayers continue till today from the haveli of Haji Mohammad Hussain, built at the spot where Ganesh Ganj Road ends and Aminabad begins, some mysterious shadows come out at the crack of dawn everyday and can be seen returning to it at sundown.
>
> (Prakash, 1995; translated by M Asaduddin)

With his famous short stories 'Khwabsurat', 'Aapbeeti', 'Ban Bas', 'Baz Goi ', 'Rone Ki Awaz', 'Bijoka' and the like, avant-garde writings in Urdu gained firm ground. Perhaps, he is the first Urdu fiction writer who sought to create fiction upon fiction. Recreating some famous characters of Premchand and Krishna Chander, he not only opened up new horizons in Urdu short stories but also generated fiction upon fiction that Linda Hutchean calls "meta fiction or fiction that includes within itself a commentary on its narrative and linguistic identity." (1980)

Surendra Prakash juxtaposes referential and evocative language judiciously and his story, 'Bhola Ki Wapsi' indicates his knack for revising the old text. Khurshid Ahmad describes it as the revisionist attitude where the old text or a well known fictional character is used as the catalyst (1988).

Surendra Prakash does not focus on any visible external reality or internal experience but he extends the story told by an old author and sometimes he gives a new life to a well-known character. Khurshid Ahmad has a point but the term he used is full of political overtones.

For S.R. Farooqui, Surendra Prakash juxtaposes violence and terror with remarkable ease and transforms non-reality into a kind of reality. He also points out that Surendra Prakash simultaneously turns attention to human tragedy and comedy and by putting on the mask of mystery, he leaves his reader completely astonished and a deep sense of frightening disquiet engulfs him. He creates a text that can be described as a vivid retelling of the story.

Another prominent progressive short story writer Abid Suhail, unlike his seniors, started a recursive and revisionist strategy of narrative embedding or multi-layered narration by providing an update on Premchand's famous short story 'Idgah'. His story also sets critifictional discourse (creating fiction upon fiction) into motion in Urdu, as it also proffers a consummate discussion on the concept of story.

His widely acclaimed stories 'Sabse Chota Gham' and 'Sawa Neze Par Suraj' depict excruciating human sufferings and sorrows in a refreshingly different and subtle realist mode of story telling. 'Sawa Neze Par Suraj' is a poignant illustration of the impact of the riot and in this story, events, characters and dialogues are made artistically subservient to the pre-ordained form of the art.

Disintegration of the joint family, the changing pattern of social intercourse and the dichotomy between traditional value systems and individual aesthetics have been delineated with telling effect by Jeelani Bano. Her famous novel *Aiwan-e-Ghazal* concentrates on various hues of family life and its cultural aspirations. The cultural ethos of South Indian Muslims is depicted astutely.

Her seemingly realist narrative dispassionately moves away from the aesthetic comforts of family life. An excerpt from her story, 'Ajnabi Chehre' unfailingly proves the point:

> Now take the case of Choti Aapa; is there any real difference between her and Badi Aapa except that Badi Aapa is slightly fairer? Of course she is much fatter than Choti Aapa and has to be weighed in 'mounds'... But Nammu could not tell one from the other. She only remembered that Chhoti Aapa always drew pleasure in afflicting pain on others. Nammu could identify them only when she heard them talking to someone.
>
> Otherwise, Choti Aapa's nose seemed to jut out of Badi Aapa's face while Badi Apa's eyes seemed to peer at her from Choti Aapa's head..........Now, how shall I address her - Choti Aapa or Badi Aapa? Only Allah knows how people remember all these faces with their distinct features. How much space is there in a small brain that they could arrange the faces in separate shelves as books in a library?
>
> Nammu often worried about what would happen if Raza came to discover this one day. Everyone in the in-law's family world knows it. Her sisters-in-law had already been hostile to her, now they would make her life a hell. Raza himself (with whom she was deeply in love now) would regret having married her – he could have married a normal good girl instead of a half woman like me. And, now he loves me deeply. Men like him are rare who can smile each time they see you.
>
> (Jeelani Bano, 1995; translated by M Asaduddin)

Iqbal Majeed rejects any pre-ordained pattern of story-telling and he deliberately discards the traditional mode of story-telling. One can hardly notice the storyline, the linear narrative structure and the depiction of characters in his stories. Far from weaving stories around mimetic realism, Iqbal Majeed pays no attention to the thematic mannerism and depicts the unending tale of self-consciousness and self pity. 'Peshabghar', 'Pet Ka Kainchwa', 'Poshak', 'Tera Mera Aur Uska Sach', 'Sukoon Ki Neend', 'Jungle Kat Rahe Hain', 'Mufahemat' and the like, create a supple effect and they even complicate the reader's own judgment.

His recent collection of short stories 'Aag Par Baithi Aurat', published in 2010, makes it clear that the difference between fiction and reality is marginal and reality and imagination complement each other.

A noted critic of Urdu fiction, Mehdi Jafar, in his penetrating article, 'Iqbal Majeed Ki Afsanvi Manzilein' pointed out that Iqbal Majeed judiciously roped in discursive narration in his widely acclaimed story 'Ek Halfia Bayan' (1990).

In this story, one could not find predetermined characters and events. The narration makes the plot stimulating and cognizant. This story draws its sustenance from a continued discourse that dwells deep in the human sufferings. Iqbal Majeed's novels, *Namak* and *Kisi Din* have also got widespread acclaim.

Ghyas Ahmad Gaddi usually hatches psychological plots in which the conscious and the subconscious supplement each other and occasionally his characters behave in an abnormal manner. Incest surfaces in his short stories, time and again, and 'Afai' brings a brother's sexual overtures with his sister, out in the open.

Individual perception gets juxtaposed with history, culture, time and the outer reality that has obtruded itself. His symbolic stories 'NaradMuni', 'Kale Shah' and 'Doob Jane Wala Suraj' got wide acclaim.

Joginder Paul's 'Nadeed' portrays an individual's complex sensitivity and aesthetic that happens to be blind. The author deploys ironic, parodic and comic modes of narration, with an aim at calling attention to the negative element inherent in sobriety and solemnity. His stories are not drawn from sequential plots, they centre around dialogues with innovative sensibility to capture both external reality and internal emotion-stirring affairs.

His story 'Haram Be' begins:

> Why dearie - wallowing over a trifle - well, I know it's pain but it's born of your own body, not circumstanced by the jaws of a lion - Thank Mungu, you ungrateful creature. You are not rolling in a lion's belly - Be patient, crazy.
>
> But how could you be patient? If you were, we would not stay a hind: you would be a perfect woman - you know my Mwanamke so well, do not you? Even when writhing in pain, she wears a full smile. You know her smile is part of her face. Its descent from the face to the heart is so smooth. Even though her pain is excruciating, the smile abides. Yours is just functional pain and will run its prescribed course only.
>
> You know how I love my Mwanamke. My love for her knows no bounds. Yet my love is independent of me: it stays home even when I go out. It sticks to her all the time - Now listen, this won't do. While I tell, my Mwanamke, the din of your travail continues . If I were your stag, I would set you right instantly with a single masculine strike. Your mate is not man enough. If he were, we would stand straight on your legs without a fuss. You are not the first in the world to pass through this process of maternity. My Mwanamke It's also delivered more than a dozen times. What happens in this? My offspring seems to be rolling down from her womb like hillocks while her smile beams even amid shadows like verdure on a mountain.
>
> (Joginder Paul, 1995; translated by KK Khullar)

'Nazaiyda', 'Takhleeq' etc. are his widely known stories. The Mini story has found a ready protagonist in Joginder Paul, as he pioneered "Mini story" in Urdu.

Ratan Singh concentrates on retelling wistful experiences and temporal time takes up his whole attention. Time takes away all that the protagonist possesses. 'Kath Ka Ghora', 'Sookhi Tahneaon Mein Tika Suraj', 'Suraj ka Mehman' and 'Zindagi Se Door' are his popular stories.

Qadeer Zaman's famous story 'Pursa' is interwoven with a sensitive portrayal of separation and communion of the lovers who were fortunate enough to lead a happy married life. The story moves away from sensuous longing and lays bare the ghastly sufferings of ephemeral life, and various shades of feelings in the human heart are subtly expressed. His recent collection of short stories, 'Khiloane Wala' carries scores of poignant images of submerged motivations and exploration of certain prohibited areas of human desires and relations.

Certainly Surendra Prakash, Balraj Manra and Balraj Komal's writings have the bearings of the post modern self-referential fiction but Naiyer Masood has run the full gamut of uncanny experiences. The stories included in 'Seemiya', 'Etre Kafoor', 'Tauos Chaman Ki Maina' and 'Ganjafa' makes it clear that the traditional narrative that owes much to commonsensical logic no longer captures the complex reality of the contemporary world where globalisation has become the buzzword. Hatching an inconclusive and discursive narrative paradigm in almost all his stories, Naiyer Masood procreates a model for making a free play of probabilities possible. Many of his stories attest Professor Suzet Henke's remark "the post modern writer may offer us an apocryphal revision of history" (1990).

In line with the post-modern writers, Naiyer Masood constructs a narrative that mocks the very concept of the history of writing and subverts its evidence presentation process. It is essentially a parody of historical discourse. His story 'Sultan Muzzafar Ka Waqia Nawees' not only presents an apocryphal version of history, but also shows his inclination toward creating fiction upon fiction.

For him, reality itself is a story which we deliberately construct through language in order to fulfill our cultural aspirations. In this story, the narrator, at several occasions, says that he was assigned to record the construction of a tomb, which he never saw. The author turns attention to the historians who merge rumour or fiction into history in the guise of objectivity.

Naiyer Masood's narrative model hardly betrays any conclusion and the following passages from his stories prove it:

> I felt that I have solved the obscure riddle but
>
> I also realised that the solution was more vague than the riddle–
>
> (from 'Seemiya', 1982; translated by Shafey Kidwai)

> "Do you remember the house?"
>
> "I do not hark back to?"
>
> "You do recall" he said in an incontrovertible tone, "You recall the house where everything was alien to you?"
>
> "No"
>
> "Yes it was so. Do not compel me, otherwise I will start questioning. Everything was unknown and you were quite familiar with unfamiliar and strange things."
>
> "Yes, it was." I replied
>
> "That's why you look back on it. The house to which you were completely unfamiliar . Keep in mind, OK?"
>
> "All right" I said
>
> "Then where is the knowledge"
>
> "Knowledge –"
>
> "It is not good to be a stranger, helper,
>
> Perhaps for the time he might or might not have uttered my name
>
> (from 'Seemiya', 1982; translated by Shafey Kidwai)

Close on the heels of some prominent post modern writers, Naiyer Masood also batters casual realist narrative by juxtaposing paradoxes assiduously. He also ropes in functional prose that is completely unprovided with persuasion or sentimental zest. Improbable but not impossible narration judiciously used by Borges, Kundera, Marquez, etc. has also been fully utilised by this gifted Urdu writer who also bagged the Saraswati Samman and a Sahitya Academy Award. Masood's narrative mode revolves around a chain of and not fixed signifiers.

Professor Qazi Afzal Hussain, in his article 'Alamkari Ke Daur Mein Adab' has discussed a new dimension of Naiyer Masood's stories:

> 'Nature of space' is a multi-dimensional concept. On one plane it is experience of the earth represented in the text. On the other hand, it is the perception of the individual writer weaved into the story. Naiyer Masood in Urdu is a perfect example of this perception. From his first major story 'Maar-Geer' to his latest 'Taous Chaman Ki Maina', Naiyer Masood has constructed stories to describe the nature, the horror and the aspiration of the place.
>
> (Hussain, 1995)

Naiyer Masood also judiciously makes use of magic realism; he writes the story of nullity that is an integral part of human existence. Sometimes, he picks up some commonplace themes such as the failure to communicate, but his discursive narrative gives it a quaint twist.

Asaduddin aptly remarks,

> Naiyer Masood, one of the most elusive and inscrutable writers in Urdu, delights in creating a world grim and sombre, with ominous limitations. His stories are never firmly anchored in time or space. His penchant for unusual situations and creating quaint and whacky characters can be seen in ample measures in 'Sheesha Ghat'. (2004)

An excerpt from 'Sheesha Ghat' underscores the above-mentioned point:

> After keeping me with him with the greatest of love for eight years, my father, my moohbola baap, was forced to find another place for me. It was not his fault, nor was it mine.
>
> He had believed, as had I that my stuttering would stop after a few relaxed days with him. Neither he nor I had expected that the people would turn me into a sideshow the way they do a madman. In the bazaars, people listened to my words with a curiosity greater than that they displayed towards others and whether what I said was funny or not they always laughed. Within just a few days, my condition worsened so much that when I tried to say anything at all, not only in the bazaar but even at home, the words collided with my teeth and lips and palate and bounced back the way waves retreat on touching the shore. I would get so tongue-tied that the veins in my neck would swell and a terrible pressure would involve my throat

> and chest, leaving me breathless and threatening to suffocate me. Beginning to pant, I would be forced to leave my sentence incomplete and then start all over again after I had recovered my breath. At this my father would say, "You've said that I heard you. Now go on".
>
> If he could not resume my account from where I had left off, I had to start all over again. Some times he would listen to me patiently and at others he would lift his hand and say, "All right, you may stop". But if I could not begin my account from the middle, I could not leave it unfinished either, and I would grow agitated. Finally he would walk away, leaving me still stuttering, talking to myself. Had anyone seen me then, I would have been thought insane. I was fond of wandering through the bazaars and I enjoyed sitting there among the group of people.
>
> Though I could not comprehensibly put thoughts into words, I made up for this by listening closely to what others said and silently repeating it myself.
>
> (Translated by Moazzam Sheikh and Elizabeth Bell, 2004)

Besides Naiyer Masood, some young Urdu writers such as Abdus Samad, Syed Mohammad Ashraf, Tariq Chattari, Salam Bin Razzaque, Paigham Afaqi, Shaukat Hayat, Hussainul Haque, Rizwan Ahmad, Ghazanfar Anwar Khan, Anwar Qamar, Moinuddin Jeenabade, Asrar Gandhi, Shahid Akhter, Tarranum Riyaz, Anjum Usmani, Shimoel Ahmad, Shafaq, Mazharuz Zaman Khan, Musharraf Alam Zauqi, Mohsin Khan, Sarwat Khan, Nigar Azeem and Khalid Javed frequently use both modern and post modern story telling modes with equal ease.

Abdus Samad, who was honoured with the Sahitya Academy Award for 'Do Gaz Zameen', invigorated the traditional realist narrative and blended in a carefully crafted structure. His writings present a situation shaped by the ambivalent attitudes of the characters that are sensitive to the vicissitudes of the age that they belong to. Balraj Komal says, "Abdus Samad presents the human drama by invoking event, action, reaction, dialogue and description together" (1990).

Abdus Samad's characters look innocent and insecure but they frequently show incredible poise. The inevitable loss of innocence forces them to seek refuge in political rhetoric. Frequently his protagonist, despite belonging to a distinct religious minority that is being marginalised by the fascist forces, thwarts every move that is aimed at artificial harmonisation or stifling uniformity.

The gradual decimation of the age-old cultural identity prompts his characters to take up cudgel against the dominant culture of the times. Abdul Samad's *Khawabon Ka Sawera* is a socio-cultural saga which attempts to extend the limits of the individualistic novel. It also reflects the apprehensions of the minority community which has been afflicted with a tirade unleashed by the fascist forces. The hero, who joins the mainstream, also allegorises and mocks at some so called reputed personalities of the society.

His stories 'Gori', 'Musical Chair' and 'Bekar Log' depict a grim human drama that is endless in nature. His densely structured stories exude their meaning through laconic dialogues:

> Yesterday I'd gone to the animal farm. I saw more vigour in animals.
>
> Give me the address, I'll also go there. These bastards called humans do not have any vitality left in them. What's the use of wasting our time on them?
>
> One of my friends knows all about animals-which animal in what season.
>
> But we're human beings. They are no longer human. Look what they've been doing for so long. They're wasting their time as well as ours. Could not they do all this in their own homes?
>
> Oh, they're changing their clothes and putting things in the suitcase. It seems they're going to leave now.
>
> Their departure was imminent.
>
> Friends, they've actually gone. The room looks so desolate like air lives.
>
> Why did they come here? Turned out to be completely useless, the idlers. Keep in mind from now on such idlers will not to be allowed to stay here.
>
> Well, then my friend......
>
> (The Indian Literature, New Delhi, Issue No. 170)

Syed Mohammad Ashraf's multisensory narrative charted new territories in Urdu fiction. His stories are firmly rooted in cultural ethos and they try to encapsulate the vicissitudes of contemporary life and inevitable human predicament with equal poise and elation. His creative work, including his two immensely popular collections of short stories, 'Dar Se Bichre' and 'Baad-e-Saba Ka Intizar' show the writer's penchant for going beyond the familiar reality with a view to coming to grips with the extended wholeness of life.

His stories astutely modulate between the mimetic rendering of the dense particularities of the experience and time sequence. His story, 'Dar Se Bichre' is essentially a candid narrative of dislocation from the land and the author ropes in allegory, poignantly.

Ashraf, who bagged the Sahitya Academy award in 2003 for his short story collection *Baad-e-Saba Ka Intizar,* uses a new mode of story telling with a view to creating narrative mode, by plugging the semantic void inherent in the expression. He frequently superimposes allegory on contemporary situations that provide a fresh insight into the power structure and the prevalent social and moral value system.

Number Dar Ka Neela alludes to the cult of terrorism. Here also sheer human helplessness is expressed through an extended allegory but without any rhetorical rush. His multi sensory narrative is braced for tearing apart cliché-ridden language that gained currency in the era of modernism.

Not infrequently Ashraf uses sledgehammer irony to portray his characters that are trapped in the awkward predicament. His narrative abounds in mythological allusions coupled with new semantic dimensions. His focus is on reinterpretation and subversion of the hereditary myths and the creation of new myths.

Ashraf's stories are essentially rooted in the cultural consciousness of a particular linguistic minority. He picks up the themes completely devoid of romantic overtones and weaves stories around non-fictional material that is both manifold and variegated.

The historical development of Urdu as a language and its widespread aesthetic impact is allegorically discussed in his famous story, 'Baad-e-Saba Ka Intizar'. The social historicity, embedded in linguistic ambience is delegated through a character that happens to be a doctor. Undoubtedly, this story, having essay type structure, aptly intrigues one about the nature of Urdu as a language. In this story, the presiding theme is language, which is depicted through a lady who is unwell:

> On the four-poster was spread a set of expensive-looking bed sheets and duvet on which reclined that frame. She was a tall human, extremely beautiful and radiant. She had golden hair like Turkish women have, which gave no clue about her age. Her forehead was clear and she had a long and shapely nose. Her kohl-lined eyes were half-open. Despite her illness, her cheeks and lips were a rosy pink. Her lips too were half open and her pearly white teeth gleamed like stars as she breathed in and out.
>
> Fine bluish veins glimmered through the clear skin of her neck. The area of concealment below her neck was elevated into a shapely cone. Her silvery hands lay bordering the well-shaped mounds of her buttocks. On a close look at her hands and feet, the doctor noticed that the woman's well rounded hands and feet showed signs of being accustomed to hard work, though efforts had been made to keep them soft and clean. The patient's breathing was irregular. For many moments at a stretch her body would lie still only to resume her irregular breath with a sudden convulsive jerk.
>
> Standing against the bedstead was a tall man whose head was covered in a four-pointed cap. On his glowing pink, aged countenance grew a beautiful yet disorderly beard. Shadows of power and beauty seemed to flit across his eyes intermittently. His personality made one feel sometimes that he was a king and other times a fakir. The doctor stood with his head bowed at the side of the bed facing the man.
>
> (Ashraf, 2002; translated by Baran Farooqui)

Ashraf's story 'Saathi' portrays movingly, the cherished desire of putting the restrictions imposed by strong bonds of intimacy aside for a while. His stories present a sensitive vision of the contemporary life that throws artificial restrictions into wind. He astutely blends realist, allegorical and metaphorical narrative modes together and this, invariably, enhances readability of his fiction enormously.

Yusuf Aarfi's stories such as 'Safar', 'Parosi', 'Behuda', and 'Besamat Hawa' muse wistfully on the vanity of sensual pleasures and worldly glories. His characters hardly make the slightest effort to disguise themselves or pretend to be what they are not.

Tariq Chattari's stories manifest a continuous and sustained search for spatial location, which re-occurs like a phoenix. His stories are intricately weaved and attempt to lay hold of an elusive cultural terrain.

Tariq's famous short story 'Nameplate' depicts the story of a man who was intrigued by the incongruity of remembrance and amnesia simultaneously. It is a moving tale of dissipation of identity and separation. The protagonist, Kedarnath, fails to remember the names of his wife, daughter and son in-law and even his own name ceases to exist in his memory. This frightening and equally unnerving experience of 'forgetting' leaves him completely bewildered but suddenly his name flashes in his memory. This gives a new lease of life to him. Here the loss of identity and its subsequent revival becomes a far more complex and nuanced existentialist ordeal. Tariq, unlike his modernist predecessors, does not use abstract narration as a short cut to create an ambience of cultural space:

> What was her name? Cannot remember at all...Kedarnath flung away the quilt and sat up on the bed.
>
> What's come over me? Couldn't have a wink the whole night. She must have had a name. I can't remember, what can I do? But I should remember the name, shouldn't I? After all, she was my wife, my lawfully wedded wife. Seventy five year old Kedarnath rested his forehead on his palm. The countless wrinkles that criss-crossed his forehead began to throb under his aged thumb.
>
> 'Sarla's mother', he blurted out involuntarily.
>
> That's all right, but she had a name too - what was it? The first letter.....
>
> Yes, I faintly remember..... He got off the bed and moved towards the light switch on the wall, muttering, The first letter of her name... K... no, no... Well, I remember now'. His toothless wrinkled face was breaking into a smile when a bout of coughing overcame him and he forgot the alphabet.

> The room was bathed in light now.
>
> His glance fell on the timepiece. It was going to be two thirty.
>
> Timepiece? Yes! T.... no! Piece....S? ... Oh yes... I think it was S.
>
> S? No, that's Sarla's mother.
>
> Again, Sarla's mother... But she must have had a name ...
>
> (Tariq Chattari, 2003; translated by M Asaduddin)

Tariq, not infrequently, fashions an indigenous narrative paradigm that is reflected in his stories 'Subh-e-Kazib', 'Khokhla Pahiya', 'Teen Saal', 'Sheeshe Ki Kirchiyan', 'Aan Ban' etc. His story, 'Lakeer' points out the compelling ugliness of communal strife but the author does not offer any quick solution or deplores Muslims and Hindus in equal measure.

Anees Rafi's symbolic and allegorical stories get widespread adulation. His story, 'Ab Woh Utarne Wala Hai' puts one's mind on human longing for one who could redeem their destiny. Anees's narrative is always invested with tremendous possibilities of interpretation and reinterpretation.

Siddiqui Alam's collection, *Lamp Jalane Wale* presents a vivid blend of dreams, pathos and mirth, and the characters jostling with each other create a miasma of magic realism with a satirical tinge. His story 'Khuda Ke Bande' is a pulsating portrait of a prostitute whose pitiable plight is comically exaggerated in the manner in which Thackeray would have done it. His characters, drawn from various hues of life, reveal a frenzied involvement in any activity as distinct from the usual careful approach to predictable routine. 'Do Peere Fartoot' characterises a life that enables us to take interest in the trivial aspects of mundane life; otherwise, we would have experienced grimness in everything we did.

Mazharuz Zaman Khan's 'Chewnti' makes it quite clear that cowardice usually inbreeds cruelty. His latest collection, *Shoora Pushton Ki Amajgah* strives to find a sense of order in the chaos of the post-modern world. The author, with his controlled overstatements and highly suggestive dialogues, tries to kindle the spark of creativity that lies dormant within. His stories are usually characterised by an undercurrent of sarcasm, irony and pungent wit but some stories do cry for a punch that is telling and effective.

Hussain ul Haq anchors his stories on the paradoxes and conceits that one can find in mundane realities. He made a dog the central metaphor of his symbolic story, 'Khar Pusht'.

It is a story that tells a wretched tale of exploitation. His other equally powerful stories 'Neev ki Eeent' and 'Nagahani' delineate various layers of human predicament. He published five collections of stories.

Anwar Qamar seems deeply concerned with suppression and subjugation and his famous story 'Kabliwale ki Wapsi' extends the famous story of Tagore; it is a story of wishful escape from political restrictions.

Shaukat Hayat's stories, set against nativist tradition, are crowded with vanquished human beings who have been displaced in their own country. Shaukat takes delight in depicting the opposite side of life. For him, the personal is the political and the omniscient narrator appears time and again. His comments, wrapped in disparaging irony, transcend the immediacy that a recent occurrence produces. 'Madho' and 'Gunbad Ke Kabootar' are his widely acclaimed stories.

Salam Bin Razzaque, who bagged a Sahitya Academy Award, uses both linear and circular modes of narration to depict the life of people who are maladjusted to life. 'Zanjeer Hilane Wale', 'Nadi', 'Bijoka', 'Nangi Dopahar Ka Sipahi' and 'Kale Naag Ke Pujari' are his famous stories, but his straightforwardness is not to be confused with simple ordinariness.

His apparent realist narrative has a sensuous strength and fittingness. Disorder in thinking and action is the presiding theme of 'Zanjeer Hilane Wale'. He also picks up an oft-repeated theme -communalism- and depicts its futility through diffusive but suggestive imagery. Salam's creative exuberance has tremendous power of subversion, at a time when communal passions run high. His story 'Chehre' invariably substantiates it:

> The corridor of the hospital was teeming with people, speaking different languages. But he could not understand what they were saying. Probably they were the relatives of those killed or injured in the previous night's riots. There were groups of people talking among themselves in hushed tones. Someone was crying and others were consoling him. Some youths were also standing there, angry and excitable. Each person was suspicious of the other. They were some constables holding batons in their hands among the crowd. He went forward and asked a constable, 'Hawalder Sahab, where are the corpses of those killed in Ramnagar last night?'
>
> 'Why?'
>
> 'My brother was missing yesterday...I want to see...among the dead'...'Go there,' he pointed to a big iron door with grills.
>
> He advanced in that direction. An armed constable was guarding the door.
>
> 'I want to see the dead...my brother...' Before he could finish, the constable allowed him to go in. The grilled door was ajar so that only one person could go in at a time.
>
> He went inside a large room without any furniture. There were two tube-lights on. Right before him lay seven mutilated corpses.
>
> He advanced slowly.
>
> He had not seen his face clearly in the dark. Nevertheless, some idea of his features was present in his subconscious. Half slit neck, bulging eyes and wide-open mouth. He came close to the corpses. He bent down to see the face of each corpse but... he jerked up, as though he had touched a naked electric wire.
>
> All the faces looked the same. And they looked exactly like his own. He felt his leg tottering, his palms bathed in sweat.
>
> (Salam Bin Razzaque, 2004; translated by M Asaduddin)

Dalit discourse has found a ready protagonist in Ghazanfar whose creative dexterity turned an idea into the event-centred familiar material. His 'Diya Bani' has set Dalit literature in motion in Urdu as the protagonist cannot stomach the heathenism any more. The protagonist belongs to a group of people who have been suffering from oppression from generations. The harrowing tale of subjugation conjures the feeling of aversion and detestation.

Ghazanfar makes us realize that religion is not an effective solution for social ills, but a charismatic weapon for manipulating the masses. He touches the subject of affliction and pain innumerably and with remarkable zest. There is a muted aggression against the degeneracy of the underdog, the downtrodden and the outcast. It does not revolve around unwavering statements but betrays the creative urge to re-appropriate certain cultural customs which are being exploited by unscrupulous oppressors.

Ghazanfar is a prolific writer and 'Paani Kanchli', 'Kahani Uncle', 'Mam', 'Diya Bani', 'Fusoon' and 'Vishmanthan' shape the contours of contemporary Urdu fiction. His story 'Hairat Farosh' aptly betrays that uncertainty does not thwart; it rather provokes the certainty of paranoia. Here one can also see the creative use of symbolic narration.

Khalid Javed's stories are extremely sensitive portrayals of human degradation and they felicitously subsume the dominant contemporary feeling of sensation and thrill – the hallmark of post modern society. In his creative world, reality and illusion fuse, overlap, intersect and blend story line with events and characters. His characters do not strive for glory; they struggle to live the ordinariness of life. Diminishing creativity, eroding inspiration and waning success certainly more than the sense of being unloved and victimised, are the defining motifs of his short stories and no Urdu short story writer could vie with him on restyling the nature of the genre.

Some naïve critic, abounding in Urdu, describes his stories as Doomsday fiction as Khalid concentrates only on stark realities which make his stories morbid and sickening. Conversely, Khalid lays bare perennial human insensitivity with unparalleled narrative vigour. One has to realise that stark realities do have epiphanies and the author portrays this in chiseled and tactile prose. 'Bure Mausam Mein' is a very frightening and powerful story in which the narrator frequently despises himself and one can feel a strong notion of self-hate:

> One eye had started to water again. He put the dark gloves back on. In the last fortnight or so as the rain eased and some hesitant

> sunshine appeared conjunctivitis had struck the town. For the last three days his eyes had not just been watering, but throbbing too. They were small, weak eyes to begin with. Now they seemed to have disappeared into the swollen flesh and what remained was red and unsightly. The dark glasses which he had dug out from an ancient trunk to hide his eyes were a relic of his student days. At that time such glasses were favoured by a certain film star and like all his fellow students, he had attempted to imitate his hero, but now they made him look like a cheap comedian.
>
> (Khalid Javed, 1996; translated by Shama Futehally)

Khalid Javed does not attempt to find coherence and order within the anarchy that plagues our life and the protagonist does not present himself to others as infallible. His story 'Aakhri Dawat' is an unnerving story of the eternal struggle of life and death. Through the story, the narrator's version of reality gets juxtaposed with other versions of the truth and traces the narrator's preoccupation with preordained notions of the reality.

The narrator, time and again, reiterates that he has been telling a story; it is not a mimetic portrait of external reality. It is the perfect example of 'skaz narrative' in which the story is told in conversation. The distinction between reality and fiction gets blurred in his other equally admirable stories such as 'Saye', 'Rooh Mein Dant Ka Dard', 'Jalte Hue Jungle Ki Roshni', 'Tafreeh Ki Ek Dopahar' and 'Qadmon ka Noha Gar'.

Khalid Javed does not discuss abstract thoughts or philosophical propositions as some naive critics believe, he simply digs beneath what looks apparent and takes the reader to the realm of reality that cannot be comprehended by common sense alone.

Baig Ehsas tries to highlight the present state of the modern world, marked by all pervading violence, loss of values and man's basic helplessness. His characters, mainly drawn from the Muslim middle class, do not have an idealised image of themselves. Unremitting thirst for worldly things prompts Baig Ehsas to denounce exhibitionism and voyeurism. Through the stories, the author makes it clear that migration has been motivated by an ever increasing desire for growing rich overnight and that it has no religious connotations.

Baig's selected short stories have appeared in English recently. The collection titled *Twilight of the Mind* turns one's attention to the indignity lurking in dignity. His story, 'Ajnabi Ajnabi' makes sensual pleasure and self-denial the objects of single pristine look.

Sajid Rasheed infused visual effects in his discursive narration and he unfailingly weaves the tale of the ordinary man who is being exploited by all quarters including religious preachers and political and social leaders. 'Hanka' is his trailblazing story in which narration is supplemented with cartoons.

Asrar Gandhi's stories such as 'Mafamehat', 'Khaleej', 'Nali Mein Uge Paode' and 'Akhbar Mein Lipti Rotian' provide a penetrating insight into the conflicts of human passion and desires. His story 'Mafamehat' gives a new sensitive base to an oft-repeated theme which is supposed to have no scope for a new interpretation.

Rizwan Ahmad is a prolific writer whose stories do not harp on apparent reality or events as he finds it quite appropriate to discuss their intellectual connotations with a high degree of objectivity. He has three collections to his credit.

Qasim Khurshid's characters are intensely real human beings and his widely acclaimed story, 'Poster' shows a keen insight into the total human situation. The innocent child, the main character of the story, who dies unsung and unwept for, has in him the vigour to rise out of his own ashes like a phoenix. His objectivised existence is depicted with rare artistry. A selection of his stories titled, *Canvas Pe Chere* was recently published and the stories are set in the thick of the social and political realities and underscore the deceitful malevolence of a political system.

Tarranum Riyaz has published three collections of her short stories and she revived the story of human relations with awe-inspiring thoroughness. Tarranum Riyaz writes stories in the backdrop of Kashmir and the cultural aspirations of the region are sensitively explored. She also makes domestic servants the protagonists of her stories and through her female characters, she lays bare an abiding human concern. A strong sense of motherhood runs through all her stories. In her stories, such as 'Gande Nale Ke Kinare' and 'Phool Mehman Sherni', servants do not appear as servants, they depict the various hues of life.

Mohsin Khan has not written much but his stories 'Zehra' and 'Balopar' engender an unparalleled pall of gloom and despair that cast a spell on the readers.

Two of Shahid Akthar's collections of short stories, *Burf Pe Nange Paon* and *Monty* turn one's attention to the events that are very close to being bizarre. Sexual encounters are narrated in a language that is markedly bereft of sensuous thrill and the climax gives a new and equally significant twist to the story .'Monty', 'Zindagi' and 'Khak Ke Uper wali Mitti' focus on the tensions of the differences and similarities erupting from the commonplace and uncanny experiences.

Fayyaz Riffat's latest collection of short stories titled *Jahane Degar* betrays thematic variations with an element of suggestion and surprise. In his short stories, a myriad moods – remorse, angst, alienation and anxiety are explored poignantly.

References

Afrahim, Sagheer (2011) *Afsanvi Adab Ki Nai Qirat.* Aligarh: Educational Book House.

Ahmad, Khurshid (1988) *Matan Va Maaani.* Aligarh: Educational Book House.

Asaduddin, M (2004). Introduction. *New Urdu Fictions.* Ed. M. Asaduddin. New Delhi: Katha.

Ashraf, S. M. (2002) 'Baad-e-Saba Ka Intizar'. Trans. Baran Farooqui. *Indian Literature.*

Bano, Jeelani (1995) 'Strange Face'. Trans. M. Asaduddin. *Indian Literature,* 170.

Chattari, Tariq. (2003) 'Nameplate'. Trans. M. Asaduddin. *Indian Literature,* 217.

Chughtai, Ismat 'The Profession'. Trans. Abul K. M. Farooque. *Indian Literature*. Issue No. 170. November–December, 1995.

Farooqui, S. R. (2004) *Afsane Ki Humayat Mein*, Karachi: Shaherzad.

Hanket, Suzet (1990) *Post Modern Fiction: The Limits of Flexibility*. London: Routledge.

Husain, Qazi Afzal (1995) 'Adab Mein Mabaad Jadeed Kya Hai'. Trans. Shafey Kidwai. *Shabkhoon Monthly*.

Hutchean, Linda (1980) *Narcissist Narrative: The Metaphysical Paradox*. Canada: Wilfred Laurier University Press.

Jafar, Mehdi (1990) *Nai Afsanvi Taqleeb*, New Delhi: Maiyaar Publication.

Javed, Khalid (1996) 'Bure Mausam Mein'. Trans. Shama Futehally and Zakia Zaheer. Katha Prize Stories. Vol. 7. Delhi.

Komal, Balraj (1990) *Tawatur Aur Tasahul*. New Delhi: Educational Publishing House.

Masood Naiyer (1982) *Seemiya*. Trans. Shafey Kidwai. Lucknow: Adabistan.

Masood, Naiyer (2004). 'Sheesha Ghat'. Trans. Moazzam Sheikh and Elizabeth Bell. *New Urdu Fictions*. Ed. M. Asaddudin. New Delhi: Katha.

Narang, Gopichand (2009) *Sheriyat: Tashkeel Va Tanqeed,* Delhi: Educational Publishing House.

Paul, Joginder (1995) 'Harambe (An African Outcry which denotes Let's Share Our Grief Equitably and Seek Deliverance)' Trans. K. K. Khullar. *Indian Literature,* 170.

Prakash, Surendra (1995) 'Shadowlines'. Trans. M. Asaduddin. *Indian Literature,* 170.

Premchand (1988) *Deliverance and Other Stories*. Trans. David Rubin. New Delhi: Penguin Books.

Razzaque, Salam Bin (2004) 'Faces', Translated by M. Asaduddin *New Urdu Fictions.* New Delhi: Katha.

Singh, Balwant (1996) *Selected Short Stories*. Ed. Gopichand Narang. Trans. Jai Ratan. New Delhi: Sahitya Academy.

2. Post-Partition Urdu Poetry

The Indian Panorama

Urdu poetry, since its inception, has tried to capture completely, the conscious life, the cognitive life, life beyond the mundane realities, the life of desire and the anguish involved in extracting the meaning of the mundane realities that are ostensibly uncanny, macabre and sordid. Its most-longed-for genre, the Ghazal, drawing its sustenance from the sentimental and metaphysical notion of love, apocalyptic hyperbole, tenacious and multi-sensory imagery, still tweaks the curiosity of those who have panache for good poetry.

The creative dexterity and aesthetic sensibility of some great Urdu poets such as Mir, Ghalib, Anees, Iqbal, N.M. Rashid, Meeraji, Faiz, Firaq Gorakhpuri, Nasir Kazmi, Akhtar ul Iman, Faraz and Shahryar, still receives widespread adulation. Their frequent and judicious juxtaposition of solitariness and heterogeneity is both awe-inspiring and ecstatic in effect.

The Ghazal's immense popularity aside, Urdu poetry's tendency for sentimental exoticism that betrays a kind of rejoicing in pain, has prompted some critics to tear its self-collapsing and clichéd diction apart. They describe it as a body of atonal and mushy writing, bordering on a kitsch that harps on the themes regurgitated by the eminent Persian and Arabic poets of the yore.

Despite this existent polemic in Urdu poetry, if various genres of the post-Independence breed of the poetry are sifted at once, both at the level of content and form, one will be able to see how Urdu poetry, as a whole, has broken away from the grotesque subversion of the normative requirements of neo-classical poetry. It is not constrained by the theme and diction of the progressive poetics. Further, Modernism's much propagated themes such as "alienation", "despair" and "angst" have become prosaic and trite.

The post-Independence Urdu poetry, especially the poetry that gained currency in the last three decades, transcends the subjectivity of poetry that portrays doubt and restlessness. Its refreshing vocabulary not only exalts the power of spoken and unspoken words but also makes it fully alive to the shifts in culture and ideology.

The post-Independence Urdu poetry often alludes to the polarity of life. Also sheer human helplessness is expressed without any overt display of emotion or rhetorical play. This poetry has shown its penchant for assimilating new modes of expression, with a view to enchanting the readers.

Chronologically, it can be divided into three phases: progressive, modern, and post-modern. In the 40s, Marxism made its way into Urdu, with the formation of the Progressive Writers' Association.

The concept of emancipation of the human being and social realism, artistically depicted by the progressive poets such as Faiz, Makhdoom, Josh, Sardar Jafri, Jan Nisar Akhtar, Majrooh and Kaifi Azmi made a tremendous impact on Urdu poetry.

There is no denying the fact that the partition of India and the subsequent macabre reality that was the unprecedented violence and destruction, left Urdu poets frustrated, in despair, agony, prostration and suffering a deep sense of guilt. The optimistic and rhetorical tone of progressive poetry went astray. It became evident that love and faith were no longer the most cherished passions. Disillusioned with all emancipatory beliefs and ideologies, man is forced to exist.

The atmosphere of gloom and terror impelled poets to deflate the recuperative myth of poetry and that too in strong, demeaning terms. Ali Sardar Jafri, a widely acclaimed progressive poet observes:

Why can't I sleep?

Beautiful is the night
Why can't I sleep?
Day's burning glasses
Disappeared in the dark
Noises of iron cuffs clanking chains, Prisoner's heavy breathing
Indecent assaults and hurled profanities by the prison-guards,
Silence of helplessness
Waiting of silence
Drowned in the enveloping darkness.

(Translated by M. H. K. Qureshi, *Urdu Alive*, 2002: 94)

Sardar Jafri's poem reveals a savage impulse that exists beneath all human actions - the pervasiveness of evil and rampant violence. In this poem, an involuntary human action, sleep, is seen as a disease. It is not a metaphor for rest as it produces sickness as though one could go hard with the 'waiting of silence'. The whole poem seems to be an elaborate piece of satirical questioning. Unfamiliar compound expressions such as 'Iron-cuffs clanking chains' and 'Hurled profanities' deflate the heroic stature of human beings.

With sledgehammer irony, Jafri refers to symbolic figures of love poetry of the East, Laila, Shirin, Farhad and Qais and concludes with satirical and epigrammatic terseness:

Robe of Sparks

Who stands there wearing a robe of sparks?
His body crushed, blood dripping from his
forehead. It's a long time since Farhad and Qais died:
Who, a people of the world, is sentenced to be?
Stoned? Here there's no elegant beauty like Shirin
No Laila of the spring-time body
Then in whose name do these wound tulips
Bloom?
There is a madman, who still speaks in the name
of truth,

Who even yet will not bow down before deceit
and sham
Clearly, stoning is the punishment for him?
(Translated by G. C. Narang and Richard H. Robinson, *Urdu Alive*, 2001, 91)

Here the poet witnesses the intense psychological drama in mundane events. The use of rhythmic speech and easily available words makes the note of bitterness more pronounced. He pursues events and thoughts to the extent of feelings. Here the existential dilemma of the lover and his trials and tribulations are neatly depicted and documented with the marked intensity of poetic diction.

For Makhdoom Mohiuddin, another prominent progressive poet, the squalid existence of human beings creates a multitude of emotional effects. The pitiable and distressing condition of the have-nots transforms them into emotive devices that arouse in one serious meditations, often accompanied by appropriate imagery.

Makhdoom's poem, 'Andhera' (Darkness) is the first poem that blends political ideology with an aesthetic experience. The objects of nature almost get human appearances and the destitute of the earth come to bear a resemblance with them. Both are uncared for and are being exploited by the ruthless rulers.

Darkness

In the night's hand a beggar's bowl,
These flaming stars, this throbbing moon, these destitute of the earth whose deprivation is their resplendent vesture,
Also their shroud.
Ensconced in this darkness, their famished
Bodies break into wails
Their bodies, the devil's easy spot.
These wounds of civilization
Deep trenches
Spiked fences

In whose tangled cobwebs dangle human corpses
On which perch shaggy vultures
These sundered heads, hands and feet
...
I see on the night's forehead a cluster
Of jaded stars posed in aching eagerness
For the sun to blaze forth
Gloom-night's only largesse to man
What else can it offer?

(Translated by Balraj Komal, Indian Literature, 1995: 58)

The beloved is portrayed as a true companion and the love denotes a quaint quality of innocence that pleases even the Gods. In his poem, 'Toor', lovers make love, before the Almighty, who smiles upon them, causing them to lose all reticence before him. God is hardly ever portrayed in as considerate a manner, as one sees Him here.

Humanitarianism is a marked feature of progressive poets. They touch on the subject of affliction and pain. In their poems, society is held responsible for the degeneracy of the underdog, the downtrodden and the outcast. For unscrupulous oppressors, love is not an effective panacea for cultural ills, but is a charismatic weapon for manipulating the masses. Sahir Ludhianvi looks at the Taj Mahal scornfully and concludes:

Taj Mahal

The garden-tomb on the bank of Jamuna, the
Memorial
Its ornate facade, the arches, the niche excellent
All this only a display of an emperor's wealth
To scorn the love of the poor
Some other rendezvous, my love

(Translated by Naqi Hussain Jafri, *Indian Literature*, 1995: 12)

Kaifi Azmi, Wamiq Jaunpri, Neyaz Haider and some others are guided by the urge to re-appropriate certain ideas. Their language becomes more than an instrument for communication. It turns into a vestigial symbol of the staggering, painful effort to find some sense in a world of nonsense.

The majority of progressive poets made meticulous use of the 'Nazam' which is densely textured, but some poets also regenerated the 'Ghazal' and tried to capture many layers of meaning simultaneously by using evocative diction. Majrooh Sultanpuri ropes in unrivalled imagery to come to grips with the extended wholeness of life.

Ghazal

Going was now easier, wind had favourably turned
When hand in hand,
Together we walked;
The path was lit
By a thousand lamps

My love had blushed at my request
Want raises her head
She coyly had bent

The dark tresses covering her face
Had set aflutter
A thousand mysteries
Of nights

My exertion, my wanderings
Eventually stood me in good stead
The journey's got
So extensively long
That my feet
Were freed
Of ranking thorns

(Translated by Balraj Komal, *Indian Literature,* 1995: 23)

Here, a slew of moods – agony, pain and exultation are portrayed with rare dexterity. Majrooh Sultanpuri excels in painting a subtle picture of human sensitivity.

Besides Majrooh Sultanpuri, Jan Nisar Akhtar, Ghulam Rabbani Taban, Moin Ahsan Jazbi and some other lesser-known progressive poets extended the lexicon of the Ghazal and their efforts went a long way in proving wrong the allegation that progressive poetry is essentially poetry of unwavering statements.

Modernism's much-touted espousal of the 'emancipation project' that was aimed at ushering in a new era of hope, prosperity and various human developments in all spheres of life, went adrift. Human life became subservient to an unremitting strife for success. Happiness too has been made a commercial commodity. An all-encompassing commercialism has usurped all other values. This has prompted some thinkers to declare that progress is a myth.

Poetry went inward and resulted in a quest for some streams through which inner reality and its complex interplay with the outer world, might seek expression. Poetry committed to modern sensibility made its appearance in the early fifties. It owes much to Meeraji, N.M. Rashid, Akhtar ul Iman etc.

Akhtar ul Iman changed the course of poetry, as his poems betray a definite deviation from progressive poetry. From the scrap of progressive poetry, he repudiates the mannerism and the feigned morality. His poignant style aims at inflicting a lethal blow on our pre-occupied notions of human behaviour.

While yoking the most unlikely things together, Akhtar ul Iman strove to avoid self-indulgence. He is also described as a poet of lost innocence as his themes are drawn from nostalgic and wistful experiences.

In Akhtar ul Imam's creative world, all things appear not as diffused narrative but highly focussed ones. His densely textured poems, replete with visual and aural images gradually exude their meaning.

His famous poem 'Ek Ladka' is about a boy, who is scorched by the blazing sunshine of memories and the inflamed boy becomes a significant metaphor of human conscience. The experiences are retold through a collage of images and filigreed word pictures envelope the mindscape, which reveals what the external reality conceals:

The Boy

On the hills beyond hamlets in the east,
Sometimes in mango orchards, or on dykes,
In lake-waters, in lane
Sometimes amidst half-clad merry-making urchins,
At dawn, twilight, in the darkness of the night;
Sometimes at fairs, with theatre traps, in their camps:
Sometimes lost on desolate tracks, chasing butterflies,
Or peering into the nest of little fledglings;
Barefoot, through burning sand and blizzards,
Fleeing from village and school, who shine,
Sometimes in happy abandon among pretty girls the
Same age,
Sometimes restless like a whirlwind, eyes bloodshot,
In dream, floating in the air, a fugitive clad
Hanging from tree branches like birds
I see a boy wandering, independent, carefree
Life - the flowing water of strong mountain springs
As though it were my shadow
As though I am a fugitive from Law
He asks me 'so you are Akhtar ul Iman?'
....
As the boys, I flare up and say:
That unhappy, thoughtful and restive self
You persistently address to, is long dead;
I wrapped him with my armbands
In the strand of self-deception
And laid him to the grave of his desires;

I tell the boy that the spark
That thought to burn the rot of the world
In a huge bonfire, has long been dead;
The boy smiles and says quietly;
That's a lie, pretence, a fib
Look! I'm alive.
(Translated by M. Asaduddin, *Indian Literature*, 1995: 13)

In this poem, the poet depicts cross currents of emotional feelings with remarkable ease. A stolid narrator is piqued at the dilemma of being; his presence has become a question mark even for himself.

Akhtar ul Iman is the first Urdu poet who meticulously makes use of interior monologue, blended with unrivalled imagery. His widely-acclaimed poems such as 'Ek Ladka', 'Yaden', 'Mufahamat', 'Takhleeq', 'Kale Safeed: Paronwale Bagle Ke Sath Sham' bring out his deep-rooted optimism despite being trapped in an awkward predicament.

G.C. Narang, the eminent Urdu critic, describes him as a thematic trendsetter:

> He has set the thematic direction of the contemporary Nazam with his emphasis on philosophical humanism. In addition, he has influenced others with his use of monologue as a mode which continues to characterize his work. (1991: 76)

Waris Alvi, while analysing the theoretical and syntactic levels of Akhtar ul Imam's poetry, arrives at the conclusion that he invented a style that could encompass the sensuous, emotional, moral and social experiences. Because of the very width of the poet's thought and feeling, language and style, the stream of his poetry has not dried up, like that of most of his contemporaries.

Apart from Akhtar ul Iman, Mohammad Alvi, Qazi Saleem, Shahryar, Balraj Komal, Nida Fazli, Ameeq Hanfi, Zubair Rizvi, Waheed Akhtar, Prem Kumar Nazar, Mughni Tabassum, Adil Mansoori and Kumar Pashi bring into focus the metaphysical depth of life with prophetic insights.

Their language is not only startling, symbolic and original, but it also cuts across all levels from street talk to academic discourse. Sometimes, they use a vocabulary emanating from a language, which is somehow, not the same as that which one is used to.

Balraj Komal, a Sahitya Akademi Award winner, posits objects that seem to lay midway between the wholly literal and the symbolic. His poems make it clear that the intricacies of thoughts and feelings require an equally oblique and elaborated use of language:

The Sunshine Stood Stripped

Who are these people?
Who wash in rain?
The clipped wings
Of doves?
For long
They gaze through windows
And bemoan the years
They eventually lost
The suckling baby
Chuckles
Grew up
And looked grave!
Though hardly tired,
He dozed off
On wings of dreams.
When it ceased raining
Sunshine in an instant
Stripped itself in distant houses,
Shores, and valleys;
The fabric of her flesh
Has a blemish of distrusting offspring
And blood,
Fouled by vagaries of yore.

(Translated by the poet. *Indian Literature*. 1995: 34)

Balraj Komal's poems, 'Ek Haath Ki Taali', 'Circus Ka Ghoda', 'Deemak', 'Braille', 'Ghubar Alood Aasman' and 'Ek Shahr Ko Dekh Kar' et cetera aptly betray that uncertainty doesn't thwart but rather provokes and promotes the certainty of paranoia. He uses a language of modulated rhythm and sonority:

Termite

It crawled into our home so
Surreptitiously and quietly
That doors, windows, tables, chairs
Books, clothes
Children's play-things
All were gone in a couple of days
The worn-out walls and roof
Came crumbling down
In consequent ruin
And lay in a heap

(Translated by the Poet, *Indian Literature,* 1995: 34)

The title of the poem 'Termite' is quite suggestive as it is not just a symbol of fast-moving time, it also turns into a grieving witness of the things once cherished by the sensitive poet.

Mohammad Alvi, another Sahitya Akademi Award winner, explores the poetic possibilities of slang and pidgin language and forgotten metaphors. He lays emphasis on the physical existence or concreteness of things which denote 'innocence within' (Dryden) and this is unparalleled in Urdu poetry. His poems shape the contours of contemporary Urdu poetry. His short laconic poems are often cryptic, fragmented and even unfinished in that they invariably reflect, in rebellion, against the contemporary "market economy".

He judiciously makes use of mushy, buzzing words – sibilants, fricatives, vowels and semi-vowels. He sits shyly on non-lexical words. The poet strives for a new kind of freedom; restlessness, hesitation, strong disapproval, alienation and mourning are necessary elements of that freedom.

Insensitive man emerges as a symbol of the moribund feudal structure:

The Angel

And God said

There has been too much of warship

Go to the earth

And see

How man is?

I came down

And was on earth

People said

You have come very late

Here now

There is no loaf of bread left

Nor is there any God –

(Translated by Bhupinder Aziz Parihar, *Indian Literature*, 2001: 75)

Words can say nothing and thus they cannot bring about any change. Alvi can thus say nothing and he does accept silence; silence portrays injustice, cruelty, sufferings and suffocation.

The stifling silence does not prompt the poet to long for death; in fact, he seems quite desperate to keep his story from getting erased. By writing 'Epitaph' the poet peels away layers of vacillating experience, accumulated over years

Epitaph

As soon as I reached the grave

I stretched my limbs to rest

And thought

And no one will disturb me now

These two yards of land

Are mine, mine alone
And so I kept mixing with the soil
And even lost the count of time
I thought at last I was at rest
But soon enough
My ease was snatched from me
It so happened
That I had not yet become soil
Somehow another person
Entered my grave
And now someone else's epitaph
Is engraved on my grave

(Translated by Anisur Rahman, *Anthology of Urdu Poetry*, 1997: 78)

Here one can also see a double desire to cease – including ceasing from memory and also a ceasing beyond ephemeral existence. Alvi also employs pseudo logical vocabulary in poems that open imperatively. Sometimes his poems seem boastful, sometimes self-deprecating but always witty.

Shahryar's Ghazals and Nazams are unfailingly infused with the pain inflicted by haunting reminiscences, as the past, interspersed with a free-flow of cross-cultural streams, enkindles his imagination. Sometimes he seeks refuge in skeptical questioning of the existentialist tradition in his creative world. There is an eloquent silence that manifests itself in a transitory dream-like situation.

The primal myth of creation has been touched upon innumerable times by Shahryar. The illusory picturesqueness of life is depicted through a central motif, that of the 'Dream'.

For him, night does not denote darkness; it paves the way for creation. Like the umbilical cord, the 'dream' binds everyday experiences, that too without false poeticism:

The Doorway to Dreams is closed

The night
Has unfolded
A new crisis for me
It emptied my eyes of sleep
And filled
The sockets with tears
And whispered into my ears:
You have been exonerated
Of all crimes,
And henceforth set free
For all time,
Go wherever you wish
Awake or asleep
The doorway to dreams is closed

(Translated by Naqi Hussain Jafri, *Indian Literature,* 1995: 35)

The Romance of Today

Distances have not yet winked,
The dream-house is still safe
From the flames of failures and disappointments
Let the tales of the coming down remain untold.

(Translated by Naqi Hussain Jafri, *Indian Literature,* 1995: 36)

For those who have given up dreaming?

When the calm river slowly came to life,
The people in the paper boat jumped with joy
Sand-soiled hands on the shore
Gathered their dreams up in handkerchiefs
And returned to desolate towns

(Translated by Baidar Bakht and Leslie Lavingne, *The Gateway to Dream is Closed,* 1993: 67)

These poems are highly obscure. The outstanding impression they leave, is that of benightedness. They are quite unfamiliar and unlike anything any other Urdu poet has ever written.

The poems are not about the suspension of reality but there is an appalling comment on all the panic and despair, which finds vivid expression in his poetry.

Shahryar's insistent reference to 'dreams' seeks to erase the difference between text and experience. It is quite evident that a considerable amount of effort is required for an experience to become a poem. The central motif of the 'dream' seems to have been crystallized deftly, from a variety of experiences.

Nida Fazli's poems are characterized by the use of speech rhythm, prosaic words and ironic posing. His narration is heightened by the use of concise and pithy phrases that linger long in the memory.

Not only does it expand the lexical and syntactic range of language but also attempts to raise the existing vocabulary. His strongly evocative poems betray a sustained aesthetic appeal inherent in mundane experiences. Nida Fazli's poetry is suggestive of the formalist tradition, in line with which, the poet sees the human emotions as an object with an inherent element of unpredictability.

Parting

When I took leave of her

She didn't say a word

But when I opened my bag

At the airport

I found

She had quietly placed

Photographs of her two children

Underneath my clothes

She is my younger sister

I wonder

Why she had

Blessed me

Like a mother

(Translated by Balraj Komal, *Indian Literature* 2001: 78)

Salahuddin Parvez hatches an inconclusive, non-discursive narrative paradigm in all his poems. He provides a model for making a free play of probabilities possible. Sometimes, trenchant comments are communicated in a comic and playful manner. His poems abound in political and social allusions. He excels at wiping out the miasma of political hiccups and bureaucratic dishonesty. The thought that pervades through his poems is an ever-growing awareness of the things "that are lost" but that still cause unbearable pain. The acute sensitivity of the poet makes him see what ails the capital of India.

Whenever I come to Delhi

Whenever I come to Delhi

I lose my real self.

Good words part company with me

I get to see the concrete of the Parliament House

That wrestling arena

Of bureaucrats and leaders

In this concrete space there no men

No women, no boys, no girls

Just the ash of words, the newsprint of a few promises

And same splinters of laughter littered aroma.

(Translated by M. Asaduddin, *Indian Literature*, 2001: 65)

Here, the narrator of the poem seems to be a trenchant critic as he exposes the wound of the city, inflicted by the corrupt politicians and by the underlying hypocrisy. The panorama of injustice, callousness, suffering and cruelty engulfs the capital city.

Bani, Zubair Rizvi, Kumar Pashi, Prem Kumar Nazar, Zafar Gorakhpuri, Aziz Qaisi, Shaz Tamkinat, Mughni Tabassum, Irfan Siddiqui Mushaf Iqbal Tauseefi, Shafeeq Fatima Shera and some others, present a situation shaped by ambivalent attitudes of contemporary society. They invest traditional symbols with new semantic dimensions.

Besides the Nazam, the Ghazal too has undergone poetic innovations both in form and content. The Ghazal has started modulating between the mimetic rendering of the specific particularities of the world and the poeticisation of experience.

Individualistic modernism, completely devoid of social concerns and nativity, was propagated in Urdu, vigorously. Further, out-dated and worn-out literary standards have been roped in to remove the poets from social responsibility. In thematic terms, 'alienation', 'despair', 'angst', 'introspection', 'anguish', 'uprootedness', 'skep-ticism' and 'disillusionment' are made the distinguishing features of modern Urdu poetry. The use of a romantic tone, based on monologue, introspection and the depiction of individual, personal experience became the hallmarks of modern Urdu poetry.

Ameen Ashraf, Irfan Siddiqui, Ambar Baharaichi, Sheen Kaaf Nizam, Jayant Parmar, Aziz Parihar, Wali Aasi, Ali Zaheer, Shahid Kaleem, Alam Khurshid, Mahtab Haider Naqvi, Obaid Siddiqui, Shariq Kaifi, Tarranum Riyaz, Shahnaz Nabi, Farhat Ehsas, Rashid Anwar Rashid, F. S. Ejaz, Abdul Ahad Saaz, Aziz Parihar, Rukhsana Jabeen, Jamal Owaisi, Khalid Ebadi, Shoeb Nizam and Shahab Akhtar impregnate their poetry with social concerns that encompass humanity at large. Modernism has suffered scathing criticism.

The emergence of structuralism has made us realise that language is not a transparent medium; on the contrary, it is not even a medium – it is a form aimed at constructing the world, consisting of things and persons. It becomes operational only at the level of differentiation. The style of these poets is consciously different from the individualistic tone of modernist poets, while still remaining felicitous.

Jayant Parmar has introduced 'Dalit poetry' in Urdu and he conjures up feelings of aversion and detestation. His poems are characterized by the use of colloquial diction and are also filled with the voices of oration, arguing and exhorting.

Jayant deliberately rejects orthodox poetic restrictions and also assiduously uses words normally taken to be non-literary. His pidgin language makes a distinct departure from the traditional poetics.

Sheen Kaaf Nizam presents the dialectical relationship between concealment/ostentation and intensity/reticence, in the chain of oxymoron.

The Manuscripts are Lost

The Manuscripts are Lost

Wherein the whereabouts of the birds

As yet unseen

Had been mentioned

Wherein-

We had jotted down

The whispering of the flowers

The mysteries of the mountains

And the bubbling of the waterfalls.

Wherein-

Deep within had been recorded

The enmity of the sun and the sea

Else

There had been scribbled

The close kinship

Of the birds and the trees

All that accentuated

Our evolution

Step by step
The manuscripts have been lost
Misplaced
Now
The lexicon is annoyed with us!
(Translated by T. S. Naseem, *Indian Literature*, 2001: 110)

The poet has lost real words, images, symbols, metaphors, etc... and now he laments that the words could be assembled and formed into poetry on the intellectual plane, without the fusing of any emotive content. The loss of the manuscript pushes the narrator of the poem into a vortex of the unknown and his vocabulary is made to look even sparser.

Mehtab Haider Naqvi's latest collection *Mawira-e-Sukhan* (2008) betrays the poet's penchant for focussing on eternal verities with a marked exuberance of expression. Naqvi, unlike his contemporaries, invests familiar symbols of the Ghazal with new semantic dimensions.

Khalil Mamoon, who has equal command of both the Ghazal and the Nazam tries to unravel a unified vision of human predicament and strongly disapproves of the false literary assumptions and so called literary values. Khalil's poems deride hypocritical social and moral values. His recent poems are replete with references to death which makes it clear that the physical departure from the world does not terminate one's journey, as the protagonist continues to exist in his creative world, which is not ephemeral. Khalil essentially belongs to the tradition of cerebral poetry popularised by Iqbal, N.M. Rashid, Akhtarul Iman, Ameeq Hanfi and Shahryar and his poems denounce the imagined past and futuristic creative utopia.

Khalil deliberately avoids self indulgence, sentimentalism and initial responses wrapped in statements. He tries to dramatise the whole narration, as the contradiction inherent in reality can only be exposed through dramatised presentation. His poem "Khamoshi Sab Se Behtar Nazam Hai" (The Best Poem is Silence) clearly sums up his basic concern:

Best Poem is Silence

In the noise of voices
In the unwanted repetition of words
In the mystery of human emotions
Best poem is silence
That listens to all rubbish
But does not say anything
Bears the brunt of lie words and meaning
But always remains silent.

(Translated by Khalil Mamoon. Unpublished.)

Ambar Baharaichi internalises the aroma of the soil and infuses some sort of a mythical dimension to mundane experiences. One can hardly find any trace of pretentious poeticism or contortions of syntax; he deftly deploys folk tradition in his poems. Portrayal of choice conflicts and cross currents of emotional feelings, masked as allegorical pictures is the hallmark of Ambar who was recently awarded the prestigious Sahitya Akademi Award. He points at the landscape vividly:

A Green Pigeon on a Dried up Branch

Birds of a feather
Sit charmed on branches
Merrily flowing winds
More fan like – refreshingly soothing
All around
We have unripe golden figs
There is a sweet water lake nearby
The weather does not make chess like move now
No hunter ever ventures
In this neighborhood

God knows
Entwined in the affectionate
Arms of the green forest
What rained late in the night?
On the heart
That the green pigeon
Sits lost
Still and quiet
On the dried up branch
Of a far removed
Lonely banyan tree

(Translated by M. Asaduddin, *Indian Literature*, 2001: 44)

'A Green Pigeon on a Dried up Branch,' tells the story of an individual who feels disgusted with the violence of disorder and the gradual loss of creativity.

Shafeeq Fatima Shera's poems carry a distinct stamp of cerebration as she scoffs at the physical condition of an anguished soul, continuously repressed and quite often left abandoned by the phallocentric society. However, her pungent sarcasm never recedes into self-pity. Her widely acclaimed poems, 'Ae Dil', 'Sada ba Sahera', 'Khiraje soat o Sada', 'Geet sandesa' and 'Silsele' unfailingly betray elemental optimism though the denunciation of gender injustice and romantic excitement becomes quite visible. The two collections of her poems, titled *Afaqonawa* and *Gillae Safoora* are deeply rooted in religious sensibility and are replete with allusions. They echo and re-echo memories and symbols with awe-inspiring aesthetic pattern.

Her diction seems powerful without being florid. We find the glimpses of an intellectual feminist spontaneity. In line with the feminist canon, she powerfully refutes the notion that attributes dull wit and timidity to women. For Qazi Afzal Hussain, Shera consciously blurs the distinction between autobiography and history, as a result of which, one can see a remarkable blending of an external and inner reality, individual and collective consciousness (*Indian Literature*, 2001: 38). 'Bazyabi' and 'Zawale Ahde Tammana' are endowed with deep cultural perception that makes it clear that culture is the most effective means of redemption.

The poem, 'Bazyafat' neither merely refers to a historical allusion nor is it invested with autobiographical references. It unfolds the intricate emotional fabric of the narrator. She has a rare ability to fathom the human mind and she meets the incongruities and ironies of life with a sense of satire. The variegated experiences of life provide her with a new realisation of the innate nature of human passion and its perverse extremes.

Her poem, 'Sadaba Sehra' sublimates the emotional instinct, making it non-individual and it also gives an impression of formalistic refinement and perfection. Sensuous imagery, satirical quips and impassioned introspection, sum up her creative world. She cannot stand sham and hypocrisy, hence she finds it quite handy to take refuge in obscure idealism. Her recent poems, 'Global Warming' and 'Qaseedae Nazmia' juxtapose trivial mirth with an innate adoration for life.

A sense of colour is most apparent in the poems of Shaista Yusuf but her poems go well beyond the intense lyricism as she has an uncommon power of creating a strange collocation of words that somewhat heightens the spirit of the comic that lurks behind every experience. Her second collection *Sooni Parchaiyan* unfolds the stories of bleak lives and silent sufferings with remarkable ease. Unbridled and tempestuous anecdotes with racy piquant flavour are consciously kept at bay and her many poems including 'Bulawa', 'Sab Behre The', 'Bazgasht', 'Rang Zone', 'Farebe Aarzoo' and 'Havas' are endowed with a subtle sense of the ludicrous and the occasional mystic flights lend an aura of enchantment to her poetry.

Obaid Siddiqui's poetry unfolds a passionate deliberation on a lost idiom as his poems and ghazals subtly touch upon love which is gradually waning as a central theme of poetry. His first collection betrays an audacious originality and experimental exuberance, and it gets immediate notice and approbation in literary circles.

For Khushbeer Singh Shad, poetry is a process of exaltation and man has no mainstay; he sinks into the abyss of nothingness.

Abdul Ahad Saz's poems, loaded with pristine myths, look at contemporary social, 'ethical' and political problems, critically and rationally, and they are never flippant or coarse.

Ali Zaheer is fully alive to the futility of making sense of a world that is on the brink of insanity and his tautly composed poems cast fresh light on incongruities of life, betray an outrageous and unsentimental disregard for the order of things, pushed forward by the so called saviours of the society. His poems such as 'Khudnavisht', 'Chehre' and 'Takmeel' expose the human weakness, masquerading under the garb of religious or ideological regimentation. These poems acquaint the readers with the queer mockery of destiny, and the candour and unexpected wit leave the readers in a whirl of enthrallment. Most of his poems are a disguised chronicle of lived experience.

In his poem, 'Khudnavisht', the poet envisions the passing away of a relentless quest for appropriation but the fragrance of the sweat of one's brow still raises the spirit of the protagonist. The poet does not conjure up anti-establishment feelings any more, as this sort of emotion seems to be fully measured up of the demand of market. Ali Zaheer's picturesque description occasionally reduces the element of lyricism and romantic vigour and increases intellectual speculation on human destiny.

His poems are remarkable in content, fuelled by the elemental human predicament and a growing ideological chasm, chaste in diction and sustained in inner life, appears quite regularly in the reputed literary journals of the subcontinent.

Alam Khurshid's veering away from the beaten path of modern poetry opens up new vistas for creative usage of language. Human sensitivity along with intricate word pattern creates a state of pensive introspection. Through his poems, he turns one's attention to the basic truths of life and these truths present a variegated mosaic of life. His 'Abad Ka Safar' (Journey to eternity) begins from the embers of burnt out romance that is depicted through metaphorical resplendence:

Journey to Eternity

I do remember
That fateful moment
When I had set out
On my journey of eternity
Through that burning desert
Someone had informed me
There flows a river of sweet water
On that side of the desert
You'll get your thirst quenched
There will be no sign of fatigue at all
That fateful moment
I do remember as yet
And since that day
I have been treading live belching sand
Facing every blow of
The burning sun with smiles.......

(Translated by M. Q. Khan. Unpublished.)

Khursheed Akbar creatively uses a diction that draws on the poetics of the protest poetry with a view to turning attention to the incongruities and contradictions of modern life. For him, complete purity can only be achieved if one makes use of a dustbin. His poem 'Dustbin' is an excellent example of satirical posing.

Dustbin

And I have come to this point
That in the form of those

Innocent little wishes
Having kept those daughters
In the heap of some rupees
Taken by loan
Any day
I will put in the dustbin
Of the body of politics
Which is like a prostitute
This is the only way
Of complete purity

(Translated by Md. Salim)

Fay Seen Ejaz's poems are marked by a certain kind of adroitness and agility. He is piqued at the routine life and the narrator believes that most people are afflicted with a blindness, a deliberate refusal to see beyond the mundane life and man must still await a Messiah to save him. 'Subh' symbolises a redeemer:

Me and my verses
Are crying out
Obstinately since long
Both turn around from side to side in uneasiness
Umpteen times we've tossed and turned
During the disorderly sleep
We're divided in hundred squares
The snake swallows us
The ladder takes us to the top
Thus emerges the dawn

(Translated by Samir Mukherjee, *A Fairy in the Goblet*, 2000: 13)

Qamar Adeeb's creative dexterity manifests itself through his painting of scattered landscapes with the intensity of sentiments and poetic diction. His landscapes reveal life in all its complexity and serene scenes bring in spiritual tranquility:

Mum

What a barren beauty

Of a house

Life

A well of loneliness

A havoc beneath the 'Dust'

A deep well of silence

Around the lips

Keep not mum

Make a sweet sound

After a long stop

Open the 'Door'

(Translated by the poet, *Whisperings*, 2010: 11)

Shamim Tariq's densely textured poetry tries to reconcile all the 'contradictions' inherent in aesthetic experience and turns attention to incorruptible values of human sensitivity.

Aziz Parihar posits himself beyond the status quo and contemplates the inevitable in the repressed voice. His seemingly labial imagery has been more poignant and heart-rending:

Joy of a Myth Displaced

I don't wish her to return

Her return means

The return of an era

Hoary with antiquity

I am a saint

Forgiving

Forgetful

Lost in oblivion

Chewing on time, change and death

A stoic

How can I betray

What lies so close?

So familiar

A myth displaced?

(Translated by the poet. *Urdu Alive*. 2002: 86)

Tarranum Riyaz denounces the ego-centric obsession with the self and regards the beloved as a vehicle in search of truth and the didactic element is too visible:

The Compromise

More often than not

The two remain lost in their words

Resting on their sides

They pretend to sleep

He gets up

Lights a cigarette

She for her part lies still

After a while

She gets up

Takes some water

He fakes snoring

This goes on and on

Morning comes

She dips herself in smile

Carries tea in her hands

He utters a word of praise as if pleased

At breakfast

Amidst the children

They seem happy

All very happy

This is the time

When both crawl out of their shell

(Translated by Bhupinder Parihar, *Indian Literature*, 2001: 114)

Shahnaz Nabi's poetry depicts feminist sensibility by denying the legitimacy of dichotomies inherent in everyday experience because there are always exceptions. Nothing is to be accepted and nothing is to be rejected. His poems go beyond individualised understanding:

Contradictions

The experiences of relations are so strange

I do not permit them to apply ointment

On my wounds

Who see my bruises naked?

Those who look at my cracked mirror

With agony and compassion

I do not let their hands grime with dust

The persons to whom I place my problems

Are not expected to solve them

(Translated by the poet. Unpublished.)

Through the drudgery of mundane life, Sharif Kaifi hears the distant drumming of destiny, where a divided self is at war with itself. His latest collection of poems 'Apne tamashe ka ticket' (Ticket of one's own spectacle, 2010) exudes a strange mixture of the serious and hilarious, the fierce and the diffusive and the poet meticulously guards himself against unbridled and tempestuous outpourings.

Not overladen with expressive idioms and emotional extravagance and exaggeration, Shariq turns the spot light on the shadowy and shady deeds of the so called enlightened man. He has a rare sense of the comic in times of tumult and turmoil. With an even-handed sympathy for the naïve and the eccentric, the narrator never shies away from poking fun at himself, and self-derision along with nipping satire enlivens the experience. For S.R. Farooqui, it is the most redeeming feature of Shariq's poetry and he observes,

> We are aware of the poems in which the poet mocks or scorns at him but Shariq's distinct ability lies in introducing himself as an ordinary man without putting on a false front. His ordinary man is fully alive to his weaknesses hence he looks extraordinary. It is unparallel and unique that he narrates his follies and shortcomings in a language that makes no effort to rationalize it.
>
> He makes a simple statement before us and unlike most of us he does not defend his imprudence and he is also not interested in explaining the real cause. Shariq's first person narrator is so implacable that he jeers at the theme of suicide and he simultaneously looks upon those who committed suicide as stupid and triumphant.
>
> (Farooqui, 2010)

Farooqui also points out that Shariq's poetry hardly touches the oft-repeated theme of love though some poems do depict the inevitable loss of love.

His latest collection, carrying about one hundred poems, portrays man caught in the pitfalls of life and his lackluster surroundings. The poet no longer believes in medieval optimism and the poet's understanding of human sensibility looks infallible.

The above-mentioned poets harp on nativity and as a result traditional and indigenous folk forms such as Doha, Mahiya, Geet and the like have also become popular. Now there is no fixed theme, no regimentation and one can only see the festivity of creation all around.

References

Adeeb, Qamar (2010). 'Mum'. *Whisperings*. New Delhi: Pandulipi Prakashan.

Akbar, Khursheed (2011). 'Dustbin'. Trans. Mohd. Salim. Ahmad, 3.

Alvi, Mohammad (1997). 'Epitaph'. Trans. Anisur Rehman. *Anthology of Urdu poetry*. New Delhi: Rupa & Co.

Baharaichi, Ambar (2001). 'A Green Pigeon on a Dried up Branch'. Trans. M. Asaduddin. *Indian Literature*, 205.

Ejaz, Fay Seen (2000). 'Morning'. Trans. Samir Mukerjee. *A Fairy in the Goblet*. Calcutta: Insha.

Farooqui, S. R (2010). 'Shariq Kaifi Ki Nazmein', Preface to *Apne Tamashe Ka Ticket*. Trans. Shafey Kidwai. New Delhi: Educational Book House.

Fazli, Nida (2001). 'Parting'. Trans. Balraj Komal. *Indian Literature*, 205.

Iman, Akhtarul (1995). 'The Boy'. Trans. M. Asaduddin. *Indian Literature*, 170.

Jafri, Ali Sardar (2001). 'Robe of Sparks'. Trans. G.C. Narang and Richard H. Robinson. *Urdu Alive*, 2.

Jafri, Ali Sardar (2002). 'Why Can't I Sleep.' Trans. MHK Qureshi. *Urdu Alive*, 3.

Komal, Balraj (1995). 'The Sunshine Stood Stripped'. Trans. Balraj Komal. *Indian Literature*, 170.

Ludhianvi, Sahir (1995). 'Taj Mahal'. Trans. Naqi Hussain Jafri. *Indian Literature*, 170.

Mamoon, Khalil (2001). 'Best Poem is Silence'. Trans. Khalil Mamoon. Unpublished.

Mohiuddin, Makhdoom (1995). 'Darkness'. Trans. Balraj Komal. *Indian Literature*, 170.

Nabi, Shahnaz (2011). 'Contradictions'. Trans. Shahnaz Nabi. Unpublished.

Narang, G.C. (1991). *Urdu Language and Literature: Critical Perspectives*. Delhi: Sterling Publishers.

Nizam, Sheen Kaaf (2001). 'The manuscripts one lost'. Trans. N.S. Tasheem. *Indian Literature*, 205.

Parihar, Bhupinder Aziz (2001). 'Joy of a Myth Displaced'. Trans. Bhupinder Aziz Parihar. *Urdu Alive*, 2.

Parvez, Salahuddin (2001). 'Whenever I come to Delhi'. Trans. M. Asaduddin. *Indian Literature*, 205.

Riyaz, Tarranum (2001). 'The Compromise'. Trams. Bhupinder Aziz Parihar. *Indian Literature*, 205.

Shahryar (1993). 'The Romance of Today'. Trans. Naqui Hussain Jafri. *Indian Literature*, 170.

Shahryar (1995). 'The Doorway to Dreams is closed'. Trans. Naqi Hussain Jafri. *Indian Literature*, 170.

Sultanpuri, Majrooh (1995). 'Ghazal'. Trans. Balraj Komal. *Indian Literature*, 170.

3. Structuralism and Post-structuralism in Urdu Criticism

The epistemological and theoretical aspects of literary theories have caused them to draw too much unnecessary attention towards themselves, especially with the publication of Khawaja Altaf Husain Hali's prodigious monograph, 'Muqadma-e-Sher-o-Shaeri' (Preface to the Debate on the Nature of Poetry) in 1893. The Preface is the first book in Urdu that goes beyond the unconditional glorification of poetry and actually tries to probe into what ails contemporary Urdu poetry. Hali, an accomplished poet, biographer, scholar and disciple of Mirza Asadullah Khan Ghalib, tried to turn attention to the theoretical and aesthetic stand point of evaluating literature objectively.

In 'Muqadma-e Sher-O-Shaeri', Hali persistently puts together well established eastern and western canons for the appraisal of poetry. How does literature reflect external reality through language and rhetorical devices? What is the sort of relationship that exists between literature and individual and collective consciousness? How does poetry communicate with the reader? How does the poet along with the reader and the text, collectively give life to a piece of literature? Do social conditions leave an indelible mark on literature?

These sorts of pertinent questions are assiduously discussed in the 'Muqadma' and Hali also delineates the distinctive features of various genres of poetry. Hali firmly believes in the mimetic representation of the external world through literature and his intent on simplicity, spontaneity and true depiction of reality, enabled Urdu criticism to release itself from the bond of opinion-centred assessment.

Being an idealist, Hali believed that poetry is supposed to convey whatever exists in the real world or that which ought to have occurred. Hali does make the representation of the reality, the cardinal principle for the appraisal of literature, as it unfailingly justifies the very existence of literature; but he simultaneously makes it clear that all things preserved in public consciousness, no matter how incredible they may be, cannot be discarded immediately.

Borrowing liberally from Milton and Macaulay, Hali delineates the contours of the dynamic relationship that exists between word and meaning and concludes that it is the reader that gives life to a text; hence he also plays a vital role in creating the meaning (Hali, 1988).

Hali's insistence on an active participation by the reader in reading a text makes him something of a purveyor of the literary approach that is now known as the reader response theory.

With the publication of 'Muqadma', mimetic rendering of the external reality has become the focal point of critical evaluation and in the first decade of the twentieth century, Marxism made its way into Urdu literature and a number of prominent writers, including Munshi Premchand joined the Progressive Writers' Association.

The Marxist theory of aesthetics advanced by Karl Marx, Friedrich Engels, Christopher Caudwell and Lucas got widespread acceptance. A number of Urdu critics such as Akhtar Husain Raipuri, Sajjad Zaheer, Dr. Abdul Aleem, Sardar Jafri, Majnoo Gorakhpuri, Ehtisham Husain, Mohammad Hasan, Qamar Raees, Sharib Rudaulvi and Aqeel Rizvi made it a point to highlight the social significance of literature and for them, the text should be fully alive to the contemporary social issues. Frequent insistence on social commitment tends to ease off the grip of the romantic and aesthetic peculiarity of the art form and the progressive writers pointed out, time and again, that literature is aimed at propelling the process of revolution initiated by the teeming masses.

Criticism committed to Marxism brought the social consciousness of the author into prominence and the critical assessment of prominent authors, in the form of monographs, book and articles, left an indelible mark on Urdu literature.

Almost parallel to the immense popularity of the Marxist criticism, cultural discourse closely linked to structuralism came forth, as Meeraji, a prominent poet of modern sensibility, published a book, *Es Nazm Mein,* in which he decoded the meaning of many poems by spelling out what constitutes cultural space and how it gets translated into an enthralling poetic diction.

For Meeraji, sub-consciousness, culture and geographical landscape play a decisive role in recording and narrating one's creative experience. By putting the force on cultural identity, Meeraji sowed the seed of a new model of criticism that certainly has the salient features of structuralism (Meeraji, 1940).

In line with Meeraji, Mohammad Hasan Askari started incorporating Ferdinand de Saussure, Levis Strauss and Foucault enthusiastically in his writings, and he wrote half a dozen theoretical articles on the relationship between archetype and literature, literary tradition, tradition and metaphysics. His widely acclaimed article titled, 'The use of adjectives in literature' manifests his sustained scholarship and speculative intelligence but his concept of tradition draws heavily from religious texts. It seems to be flawed, controversial and inscrutable as literature does not necessarily complement religion. Askari deftly ropes in structuralist poetics in his several articles such as, 'Fear of Metaphor', 'Pornography in Literature', 'Use of Adjective in Literature', 'Grand Maternal Mother of Modern Women', 'Human Being and Man', 'Progressive Literature' and 'More Alluring than Tears' with a high degree of objectivity.

For Askari, a close reading of the text is not supposed to be aimed at evaluating the thematic mannerism but it has to concentrate on the "langue" of literature. He points out that the text is not just a verbal icon completely devoid of historical and ideological connotations and social underpinnings.

Meeraji and Mohammad Hasan Askari's incisive analyses relegated Marxist criticism to the second place and their writings paved the way for formalist criticism. New criticism's insistence on close-reading of the text prompted many critics to view literature as a self-contained unit or monad. Existentialism exposed the limits of emancipatory ideologies and made inner reality the object of a single pristine look. It provided a theoretical framework to modernism; depression, alienation, angst, restlessness, disillusionment and individualism became the defining themes of literature committed to modern sensibility.

Besides paraphrasing themes, many critics were looking for new ways to explain literary texts cogently. These critics adopted an extensive and focussed study of the surface and in-depth structure of a piece of literary work. Khalil Rehman Azmi, S. R. Farooqui, Gopichand Narang, Waris Alvi, Waheed Akhtar, Baqar Mehdi, Mahmood Hashmi, Fuzail Jafery and Mughni Tabassum blended new criticism with structuralism and helped Urdu criticism extricate, from the bond of theme-centred assessment that lays emphasis on social commitment in equal measure.

S.R. Farooqui's quest for universal principles of appreciating literature allows him to look at structuralism quite closely. He made Urdu knowing people realise that poetics is not just an assortment of rules and convictions related to the text but it is the 'langue' of the literature – a matrix of codes and literary convictions that set manifold cultural inter-textuality into motion. The variety and abundance get sustenance from the 'parole' that is generated by the individual creative talent. Farooqui has many seminal works to his credit and his articles such as 'Sher', 'Ghair Sher aur Nasr', 'Mutale Asloob Ka ek Sabaq', and 'Panch jaded Shair' et cetera contain critical insights, are grounded in the eastern and western canons of appreciating literature and thus are able to achieve the high point of the objective of literature. All later critics are heavily indebted to him.

With frequent and extensive use of formalist tools of evaluating literature, S. R. Farooqui made a sustained attempt to analyse the whole system in which an individual author uses language creatively. His recent substantial exegetical study of Meer Taqi Meer, titled 'Sher-e-Shor Angez' is replete with structuralist and post-structuralist insights. Having painstakingly analysed both theoretical and syntactic levels of Meer's poetry, Farooqui deflates many misconceptions and stereotypes and concludes that Meer's poetry can only be made tangible if it is placed in the perspective of the oral tradition. Meer's poetry does not sink into gloom as its apparent lugubrious diction reverberates and enraptures the reader. Farooqui makes a conscientious effort to bridge the gap between an overtly scholarly audience and a general one, for whom this work may be their first introduction to Meer's poetry. Elucidating Meer's poetry in the backdrop of human relations, he meticulously specifies the essential traits of the lover and says:

> The individuality of the lover lies in the fact that he does have all the characteristics of the traditional lover but we take him as an ordinary man. For us he is not a verbal convention and the man quite evidently looks an inhabitant of our world while the traditional lover is always imaginary and type. Neither this man of our world is Mohammad Taqi Meer nor it is a character of the fiction so that we could look for his motivations.
>
> (Farooqui, 1990)

Farooqui also tries to collate the poetics of the tales by turning attention to the semantic space, thus making it clear that the narrator of the story relentlessly tries to arrest the attention of the audience through 'spoken words' as the tales hardly have complete written texts. If Farooqui's recent writings are sifted at once, one may realise that he adopted Saussure's synchronic study of language, which, in the final reckoning, seems quite purged. His unbending adherence to the formalist criticism makes his studies completely bereft of those social and ideological concerns that pervade through the text.

For Farooqui, literature is not an intrinsic part of a wider social discourse; hence cultural concerns are hardly discussed in his writings. Conversely, Farooqui, in his fictional writings like *Swar*, a collection of short stories and *Kaiye Chand The Sare Aasman*, a novel, weaves fibula (plots) around the cultural milieu and the historical consciousness. This sort of dichotomy pervades through all of his writings and it also takes a heavy toll on his otherwise perceptive writings.

Urdu criticism's tendency to avoid literary theory has always piqued Professor Gopichand Narang and it also impelled him to probe for a well-defined and congruous literary poetics, fully alive to the cultural and aesthetic sensibility of Urdu knowing people. His literary odyssey began with the scholarly interest in new criticism, stylistics, semiotics and socio-linguistics and his book, *Karkhandari Dialect of Delhi Urdu,* with a foreword by Dr. Suniti Kumar Chatterji, was published in 1961. The book presents a focussed linguistic analysis of language used by the workers and artisans of Delhi.

Professor Narang connects Karkhandari Urdu with the deeper structure of Urdu language and its other variants with remarkable thoroughness. The style is coupled with focussed critical acumen, along with lucid and perceptive analysis that judiciously makes use of stylistics, structuralism, post-structuralism and the Eastern poetics.

History finds Professor Gopichand Narang on the right side of many of substantial literary trends and ideological discourses of the twentieth century and his books in Urdu, English and Hindi demonstrate a sharp critical insight and a deep understanding of the contemporary ideological positions and literary debates. In his writings, one can see that a variety of discourses, expressing different ideological positions are at play, without being evaluated by a totalitarian authorial discourse.

His intent on the close study of the text by employing stylistics and semiotics made him one of the gifted disseminators of new literary theories. Professor Narang's writings are not only aimed at suggesting possibilities in reading literature but they also touch upon every genre, from the Ghazal to the Masnavi, the short story to the novel and Arabic Persian literary theories and Sanskrit poetics to structuralism and post-structuralism. He deftly applied his profound learning and speculative intelligence by roping in these approaches and insights, to re-examine and re-evaluate the whole range of Urdu poetry, including Mir, Ghalib, Iqbal, Faiz, Firaq and a host of other Urdu poets.

Turning attention to Faiz Ahmad Faiz (1911-1984), the most influential poet of the post-Iqbal period, Professor Narang deconstructs his widely known poems and points out that Faiz employs classical imagery and conventions to portray contemporary social, cultural and political concerns but in the final reckoning, inherent gaps and silence of the text somewhat subvert the intended meaning. He points out:

> Faiz is as deeply concerned with purely personal themes as he is with the nationalistic and socialistic. Frequently the two emerge as poles, putting him in two different directions. In his poem 'Mujh Se Pehli Si Muhabbat Mere Mahboob Na Mang' (Love, Do not ask), he speaks of his beloved whose beauty kept 'Earth's spring times from decay' as one pole and 'men's bodies sold in street and market place ......with festered sores dripping corruption', as another pole. One is calling for love and the other for action. To Faiz, both are dear. He wants to respond to individualistic urges as well as to the call of the exploited. Hence the request – 'love, do not ask from me that love again.'
>
> The emphasis is on the words 'Phir Se', as individualism completely divorced from the plight of society, is meaningless to Faiz. This cleavage between human passions and socialistic obligations or the division of loyalty between reality and ideals, classical and modern or love and faith runs its contradictory course through the poetry of Faiz.....whenever the poet is beset with social problems and is given the freedom to speak through his conscience, he will feel the cleavage between duty and choice, the ideal and the practical. But what lends a unique quality to the quality of Faiz's poetry is the fact that besides being true to his personal feelings and writing lyrical verses of great ecstasy, he has transformed some elements of the classical poetic tradition by infusing them socio-political meaning.
>
> (Narang, 1991)

Sakhtiyaat, Pas-sakhtiyat Aur Mashriqui Sheriyaat (1993) (Structuralism, Post-structuralism and Eastern Poetics) is a philosophical and rhetorical de force of his scholarship and it is perhaps the most comprehensive and scholarly work on new literary theories to have been released in recent years. With an even-handed attention to Western and Eastern poetics, Professor Narang has divided his stimulating work into three sections, which he refers to as three books. The book not only provides a veritable overview but also offers a wealth of discussion on the concepts of language and literature and how they construct reality.

At the outset, the author rightly brings out how structuralism strikes at the roots of the metaphysical concept of reality. The apparent views about literature owe much to common sense which itself is an ideological construct and draws its sustenance from historicity, which acquaints the reader with the simple chronology of events, while letting pass unnoticed, the cross currents of human sensitivity.

Professor Narang is at his most persuasive best when he draws parallels between Saussure's sound patterns of words and concepts such as 'Psychological Phenomena' and ancient Indian thinkers' and grammarians' candid distinction between Prakrta dhvani (the Psychological) and Vaikrta dhvani (the physical). Narang connects Saussure's view that, in language nothing has any positive value except in opposition to something else, with the Apoha theory of the Buddhist logicians and thinkers who pointed out that the meaning of a word is not in its positivity but in the contra-distinction of its correlates. Such a clear insight into ancient and modern poetics can rarely be found among contemporary critics and scholars of the sub-continent.

The book attempts to set up a tripartite intimate dialogue between Sanskrit Poetics, Arabic Persian Poetics and Structuralism. Narang has concentrated on the relatively ignored Eastern Poetics with the glow of his probing mind and gleaned up early signs of contemporary literary theories from the dead past. The internal evidence is convincing in its precision and application. Having yoked Eastern Poetics with structuralism and post-structuralism, Narang initiates a rich discussion on the new model of criticism. The debate also explores the simultaneous quest for a universal and national identity. To a great extent, the author has done a remarkable job. A common strand that runs through this monumental book is the modesty and insightfulness.

His recent book *Fiction Sheriyaat: Tashkeel-o-Tanqeed* (2009) (Poetics of Fiction: Formation and Criticism), proffers a perceptive discussion on how fiction readjusts innate human impulses. A close and perceptive textual study of prominent fiction writers such as Manto, Rajendra Singh Bedi, Krishan Chander, Balwant Singh, Intizar Husain, Gulzar and Sajid Rasheed makes it clear that ideology, philosophy, history, aesthetics and linguistics constitute the cultural space from which a piece of literature draws its breath. For Narang, cultural conventions invest the text with aesthetic depiction that arrests the attention of the reader, cutting across the time and space barrier.

Contrary to the widely accepted concept of originality of the writer, Narang points out that the writer's mind is firmly rooted in history and culture and whatever he produces is borrowed heavily from previous texts. He cogently delineates that culture is not an oppressive theological and monocratic (inflexible) concept, but subsumes different and divergent points of view, attitudes and ideological aspirations. In other words, a cultural system gives birth to a text and the text produces various tissues of culture that fire human imagination.

The author also deconstructs several masterpieces of Premchand, Manto, Rajinder Singh Bedi and Balwant Singh. As a self collapsing entity, the text hardly sticks to a centre and subverts many popular beliefs. Referring to Prem Chand's popular short story 'Kafan' (The Shroud), Narang asserts that the title of the story turns attention to the binary opposition that surfaces in almost all human experiences. The title of the story, 'Kafan' (The Shroud) does not only refer to that which covers the body of the protagonist Budhiya, but also calls attention to the fact that her womb that provides nourishment to the offspring as well becomes the shroud of her unborn child.

For many critics, Rajendra Singh Bedi's stories usually become smitten with titillating depiction of sex. Professor Narang aptly explains the creative process of Bedi to understand his sexual sensibility:

> It is well known that classical Indian tradition is marked by a typical candidness when it comes to the question of sex. But the descriptions are neither titillating nor arouse gross passion verging on lasciviousness. The undercurrent is that of bliss generated by the male-female union. Seen in that light, sex in Bedi belongs to the

> ancient tradition. Passing through a maze of human relationships in their varied forms he reaches the fathomless depths of the male-female union. While unfolding the tangled strands of the interaction of physical and spiritual bliss and while listening to the throbs of the human heart, he sees man and woman so united, becoming a part of the cosmic riddle.
>
> (Narang, 1991)

Professor Narang's recent reading of many well-known writers such as Prem Chand, Sadat Hasan Manto, Shahryar, Gulzar and Jayant Parmar, makes him the chief artificer of the post-structuralist discourse in Urdu.

A number of books and articles, drawing new critical insights, such as post-colonialism, new historicity, nativity, subaltern and feminist discourse, appear frequently which also makes it clear that post-structuralist discourse has now come to fruition, in Urdu. Scores of established and new critics such as Wahab Ashrafi, Devendra Assar, Qazi Afzal Husain, Ateequallah, Nizam Siddiqui, Abul Kalam Qasmi, Khurshid Ahmad, Khalid Saeed, Qazi Jamal Hussain, Aqueel Ahmad, Anees Ashfaq, Sheen Kaaf Nizam, Mazhar Mehdi, Shikoh Mohsin Mirza, Maula Baksh and Kausar Mazhari relentlessly analyse both old and new texts, by employing new critical insights. Their readings are lapidary in which the indeterminacy of the text is always dwelled upon.

Besides the above mentioned critics, a well-known critic who espoused modernism with vigour, Waris Alvi, notwithstanding his apparent discontent with post-modernism, lays emphasis on nativity, cultural aspirations and the role of ideology in creation of meaning.

Describing ideology as the core of literary discourse, Waris Alvi in his article 'Ideology Ka Mas'ala', says that infusing criticism with technicalities of stylistics does not, in any way, make it wholesome. Conversely, it manifests atrophy. If criticism does not tell anything about human life and the world, then it becomes just a dull-witted explanation of the craft. 'Pesha To Sipahgari Ka Bhala', 'Pairvi-e-Maghrib' and 'Qissa-e-Jadeed-o-Qadeem' are his most insightful theoretical articles and the author rightly decries the sterile sloganeering of modernism.

Wahab Ashrafi, a trained formalist critic, has written a scrupulous and nuanced book, *Ma'bad Jadeediyat (Post-modernism – Implications and Prospects)* that creates a sense of epistemological and narrative cohesion by closely analysing some significant contemporary writers. The book, up to some extent, clears the ever-growing cloud of suspicion that hovers about post-modernism. The author frequently throws a tirade about those who miss no opportunity to hurl abuses at post-structuralism. Wahab Ashrafi ropes in post-structuralist insight frequently and he examines texts with an understanding but critical eye.

In one of his articles, 'Ma'bad Jadeediyat' (Post-Modernism), he cogently deflates the myth of universal truth as he asserts that one creates truth, through language, in order to fulfil his cultural aspirations. No truth exists beyond language and culture, and the very belief of eternal truth paves the way for stifling homogenisation.

Ateequallah's writings set in motion a discerning debate on structuralist and post-structuralist poetics and his analyses go beyond trendy and formulaic words and terms. 'Feminist Poetry in Urdu' is one of his most insightful articles and it proffers a serious debate on exclusive identity of women. His two books, *Tarjeehat (Preferences)* (2003) and *Tassubat (Prejudices)* (2004) mark the pleasant fusion of the author's interest as a creative thinker and a socio-lingual analyst.

Hamidi Kashmiri, an accomplished formalist critic, now focusses on cultural space and his analysis is aimed at showing the different creative possibilities of using culture as a source of inexhaustible inspiration.

Abul Kalam Qasmi, with his thorough grounding in Eastern poetics, applies structuralist and post-structuralist insights in analysing Ghalib, Akhtar ul Iman, Qurratul Ain Haider, Shahryar and Irfan Siddiqui.

Connecting the western model of post-structuralism with the Indian mind, Nizam Siddiqui refers to Dr. Ambedkar and points out that he presented a parallel model of creating cultural space which unfailingly represents the voiceless and forgotten. He also takes a dig at those who want to resuscitate traditional and classical poetics but only manage to usher in stifling homogeneity. One has to realise that the tradition does not knock down pluralism, indeterminacy of meaning and creative usage of words that modern literary theories hold dear.

Qazi Afzal Husain, in sparse, closely argued prose, with perceptive explication of the well-known Urdu authors, delineates two key concepts of post modernism – parody and intertextuality. He quickly spots inconsistencies, erosions and obfuscations inherent in the text. His articles, 'Tarseel ki Nakami Ke Baad' and 'Theory/ Literary Theory', subtly expose many misguided assumptions advanced by modernism. For Qazi Afzal Husain, Derrida is the first theorist who criticises the static and regressive nature of structuralism. His focussed and edifying reading leans on Derrida heavily; hence it barely escapes from the hagiography of Derrida.

Maula Baksh, a young Urdu critic has written a monograph on Meer Asar Dehlvi, a poet of the Eighteenth Century, in which he applied new methods of reading texts with remarkable inventiveness. According to him, Meer Asar deliberately creates text upon the text of his more accomplished elder brother, Meer Dard and his intertextual semantic space leaves the reader in awe of him. His creative retouching is endowed with unparalleled narrative fluency.

Maula Baksh has also written a book on Gopichand Narang's contribution to structuralism and post-structuralism. He frequently writes on contemporary authors from the standpoint of post-structuralism.

References

Farooqui, S. R (1990). *Shere Shor Angez* **1**. New Delhi: NCPUL.

Hali, Khawaja Altaf Hussain (1988). *Muqadma Shero- Shairi.* Delhi: Educational Publishing House.

Meeraji (1940). *Is Nazm Mein.* Lahore: Maktaba Saqi.

Narang, G. C. (1991). *Urdu Language and Literature: Critical Perspectives.* Delhi: Sterling Publishers.

4. Jayant Parmar

The First Voice of Dalit Poetry in Urdu

It seems incredible to think that a 30-year-old who uses words and a painting brush with equal felicity can pick up a language learning guide from the downtown market of Ahmedabad that is famous for "things that are not in currency" as it is the area where one hardly gets to see any shopping mall, food plaza or a multiplex. It is surprising that this is the place that makes him realise that there is a life that does exist beyond selling, buying and sensual pleasures. Soon he becomes fully conversant with the nuances and idioms of a language that is apparently incompatible with his cultural ethos, ideological concerns, his value system and religious beliefs; surprisingly, within no time, he has a command on the complicated and formidable prosody of that language. Eventually, his ever-increasing proficiency in that particular language, coupled with his creative dexterity earned him the prestigious Sahitya Akademi Award in 2009. It is not a piece of fiction, but what was achieved by Jayant Parmar. His transformation from a Gujarati poet and painter into an accomplished Urdu poet leaves many awe-struck. His poems make it clear that creativity transcends language barrier. His second collection of poems 'Pencil Aur Doosri Nazmein' got the Award of the National Academy of Letters – Sahitya Akademi – for Urdu in 2008.

Jayant Parmar who has continuously been haunted by the repugnance of hell pit admits that the atmosphere around him was hardly conducive for any creative work. Narrating his childhood experiences he points out:

> My mother was an illiterate Dalit and my father was a factory worker who never attended school. During my formative years, I realized that I have to cling to life all alone. At the age of fourteen, I took up a brush to earn a livelihood. I started selling portraits but soon got attracted to miniature paintings. I would draw miniature paintings for a frame seller, and that was the place where I found untouchability at its peak. A separate water pot was earmarked for me and I was not allowed even a running water tap. It left me completely dejected.
>
> (2009)

Jayant Parmar lived in the Muslim dominated locality of the walled city of Ahmedabad; he developed a strong liking for Urdu poetry and it prompted him to start learning Urdu.

> I picked up a copy of *Urdu Script Teacher* from a roadside bookshop and I found Urdu, the most effective medium of my creative expression. I also tried my hand at Urdu calligraphy.
>
> (2009)

Jayant Parmar first started composing poems in his mother tongue, Gujarati and then found it quite appropriate to express himself in a language that takes pride in taking recourse to sentimental exoticism. Urdu poetry, largely infused with highly suggestive imagery, conjures up multiple meanings but Jayant Parmar's poetry betrays a definite deviation as he focusses on a relentless probing into the human predicament through the prism of his intensely personal anguish which he describes as the 'smell of hell pit'.

He does not bear his sufferings lightly and peels away layers of ignominy that he had felt at having faced untouchability that had accumulated over years, in an idiom that is direct and completely devoid of rhetorical flourish.

From the scrap of poetry committed to romanticism, social realism and modern sensibility, he repudiates traditional values which we consider our most cherished possession. With his laconic poems, he tries to transcend the ideological, caste and ethnic schisms that have cursed our country. One can hear the voice of a dispassionate narrator who refuses to compose a poem on the experiences of the past or the wishful past.

The protagonist pays no attention to the beauty around him as he has continuously been dogged by the "smell of hell pit". The smell smothers his creativity and it lingers on, no matter how hard he tries to ward it off:

The Smell of Hell Pit

Used to dog me
To my school
Below the sun umbrella
It would descend
Barefooted
In the hell pit
She wailed
Wet
The animal skin
In the slut and ....
And cleanse it
With her dead feet
As a reward
For me
Pieces of meat
Even today
Before I leave for my office
When I shine my shoes
With cherry blossom
In the shining
I see my mother's face
The smell of hell pit
Dogs me to my office

(Translated by G. K. Vankar)

Here the narrator's eradication of the past produces poignant vignettes about his upbringing and it surfaces everywhere - be it in the mother's face or the shoeshine.

The memory of the mother is peppered with interminable images of indignity and 'shine of shoes' and it calls to mind, the face of the mother who was taken for a ride by the hoity-toity. Such anecdotes spurn out of control and the poet cannot put up with them. Jayant Parmar's poems question established truths, as he cannot ingest the fiendish attitude of the society. He has set Dalit poetry in motion in Urdu and his three collections *Aur* (1999), *Pencil Aur Doosri Nazmein* (2006) and *Manind* (2007) make it clear that his poetry is not being written for astral beings. His poems touch the subject of affliction and also turn attention to a savage impulse that exists beneath all human actions, the pervasive tendency to exploit have-nots. The pitiable and dolorous condition and degeneracy of the outcast makes the narrator take refuge in ironic posing, ie. satirical questioning and his clear, unclouded account is generally disguised with vituperative terms, in a language modulated by speech rhythm:

Hath (Hands)

I had asked for home

And they buried me alive

I had asked for a small piece of land

And they put a stone of migration on my head

I had asked for bread

And they put live coals on my tongue

I had only asked for a book

And they poured the molten lead in my ears

(Translated by G. K. Vankar)

The reference to some common possessions such as a book, a pencil, paper, a pen, ink, a brush and colour hardly makes one inquisitive but these commonplace belongings become the most sought after things for those who have never been allowed to use such things by the ruling class.

The simple demands of the have-nots were rejected with contempt and the seekers were severely punished. It is an appalling situation that is depicted through irony.

The author touches on the theme of humiliation time and again, and each of his poems is scorched by denial and disavowal. Presented in everyday conversational idiom, his poems on the above-mentioned themes are born as a result of angst.

The inflamed narrator no longer prates about the infidelity of the lover and his medium of expression - a pencil - suddenly turns into a grieving witness of the sensitive poet:

Pencil

A polio-stricken hand
Asks a broken blue pencil
Lying next to one foot
Can you write?
The pencil hesitates and says:
Yes, I can write
And make your pictures too
But only if
You can remove the plaster of my frail body
With the help of a pen-knife
Surprised
I keep listening to Hussain Baksh
On Zee TV
Leave the cup and the flask........
.........I

(Translated by Bedar Bakht, *Indian Literature*, 252, p. 74)

For him, the paper is not made up of leaves or pulp but it does bear resemblance with his body that is dotted with untold tales of torment and misery. Sordid tales of untouchability can only be written on the naked bodies of the Dalits and the level of indifference towards this injustice is shocking. Dehumanisation gets widespread approval and it leaves the narrator dumfounded:

Kaghaz-I

In the olden times
They used to write
On ordinary leaves
On the back of a tree
On palm leaves
On chests of palm trees
On stones
On animal leather
The four Vedas
Were also written
On the back of a tree
But the black accounts
Of tyranny
Were written
On my body
Even today

(Translated by Bedar Bakht, *Indian Literature*, July-August 2009, 252, p. 69)

Instead of the broom and scrubbing brush, the narrator picks up the pen, pencil, the painting brush and paper through which he asserts himself; he wants to get a distinct recognition for himself through these and not on the basis of his caste or profession. The pen empowers him and he uses it as a poisoned knife to tear apart the brahminically defined social system. The omniscient narrator reacts subjectively to various forms of subjugation. Now the Dalits appear as a newly created social, religious and political community (Dharnandkar, 1994).

Jayant deflates the myth of metaphoric precision of poetry and weaves filigreed word pictures with satirical and epigrammatic endings. In one of his popular poems, 'Black Poetry', the poet describes the black ink as the abode of 'the Soul of Black Folk'. Not only does the conclusion of the poem startle the reader, but also prompts him to believe that the pen betrays dark screams of the marginalised voices. For him, love is not a cure for deprivation but conversely, courtly love and romantic excess are charismatic weapons used for manipulating the toiling masses.

Casting aside the popular grandeurs of Urdu poetic diction, Jayant recollects an experience that does not indicate the slightest notion of self pity and self indulgence. In his creative world, the distinction between personal pain and abiding concern for humanity gets blurred. Death is not a physical departure but it is a form of mindscape. For the poet, death simply means a complete split up between words and meaning.

> The migration of words and meanings
>
> From the street of heart
>
> On the leaves of passion
>
> The footprints of autumn

Dalit poetry uses diction which is somehow not the same as that which we are accustomed to.

Having been subjected to the worst atrocities, the Dalit poet remonstrates about all forms of exploitation based on class, race and occupation. The poet deliberately rejects traditional poetic restrictions and assiduously conjures up the feeling of aversion and detestation. His poems are filled with the voice of oration, argument and exhortation.

His poem 'Dalit Poet Ki Akhri Wasiyat' appears to be a vestigial symbol of the staggering, painful effort made to find some sense in the world of nonsense:

A Dalit Poet

> Leaves several things behind;
>
> A paper dripping wet with blood,
>
> A black sun,

On the night's head,
A river of blood,
A lantern of his ancestors,
He never assaults you with
Symbols,
Metaphors,
Or personalities
A heavy burden on a donkey's back,
He is himself a wounded shadow
He has no existence
There is little difference
Between him and a broken cup
He who makes images with cow-dung
Has at least the sense to know
That in the hour glass
In the smell of exiled earth
In the sunflower of rebellions
In the spear of the pen and the ink
And lives forever
But now
He is looking for his existence
He is looking for himself
He is proud to call himself
A Dalit poet

(Translated by Bedar Bakht, *Indian Literature*, July-August 2009, 252, p. 81-2)

The poet lives in a society where language has become a convenient tool of exploitation, used by the ruling class to strengthen its hegemony. The poet is reluctant to make use of words and without words, his poetry becomes a question mark even for himself. It is a time for exultation, as the newly-acquired identity of a 'Dalit Poet' has made him proud. A discourse on liberation from the caste system pervades through all these poems, with an idiom of their own, which really have no boundaries, but these cannot be laid aside as complaints.

With his gleaming poetic candour, Jayant merges his poetic individuality into a nameless mass. In an unjust, moribund society, the poet is impelled to use his pen and ink as his weapons but cannot untangle the knot of human predicament. Jayant seeks a new kind of freedom that is peppered with strong disapproval, alienation and informality.

Jayant avoids obscure vocabulary, Persian idioms and compound words deliberately and unlike his contemporaries, he does not repeat himself. As Balraj Komal points out, he takes birth in his poems time and again and every time, discovers a new dimension of his awe-inspiring creativity.

The title of one of his famous poems, 'Sapne dekhne wale hath' betrays an extreme form of suppression and exploitation, as the narrator is impelled to use his hands for having dreams, as he cannot make use of his imagination. Even for that creative urge, he has to use his hands, through which he earns his livelihood. Imtiyaz Ahmad, a young Urdu critic rightly points out that his dreams ought to be those of the making of knives and daggers and the putting of heads on daggers. It is a violent protest that is unheard of in Urdu poetry.

Delineating the contours of the poetic creation of Jayant Parmar, eminent Urdu critic Gopichand Narang aptly observes:

> Urdu language is the cultural language of Muslim minority, but Jayant Parmar's predicament represents a minority within minority. In other words this marginalized voice is subaltern within subaltern. Subdued in the haze of pain, this is sigh of leaves falling in the autumn sun; In the backdrop of sad colours; poems with the themes of 'mother' shock the reader. If one could be lost into the text, one

> can discover it in words of rags of historical pains and discrimination that has been taken for granted and has been going on for ages.
>
> (2009)

Jayant also writes romantic poems but they too are meshed with his commitment to the causes that he lives for. His desire for securing an honourable place in the society and his anguish at poverty, runs through all his poems.

Explaining the symbolic meaning of the title of his second collection *Aur*, Jayant points out:

> There is an invisible mountain behind the elevated peaks. Apparent is not always the truth and I intended to go beyond it. The word 'Aur' (And) joins words and sentences and I try to bind hearts together through my poems. In my creative world, lion, bear, leopard, flavor, darkness, sunshine, seasons, paper, pen, pencil, brush, canvas, easel and man, all have their distinct identities. My symbols and metaphors are drawn from routine type. My poems do reveal a deep sense of agony and pain. One might hear in them a tone of assertion rather than a note of an apology. (1999: 7)

References

Dharnandkar, Vinay. 1994. 'The Dalit Poetry in Marathi'. *World Literature Today*, 68. p.

Narang, Gopichand. 2009. 'Jayant Parmar: Poems on the Easel'. *Indian Literature* (July-August 2009) 252. p. 68.

Parmar, Jayant. 'Qalam Daawaat Aur Mein'. *Aajkal Urdu Monthly*. April 2009, p.8.

Parmar, Jayant (1999). *Aur*. Ahmadabad: Sukahn Kada Publications.

Poems of Jayant Parmar. Translated by Bedar Bakht. *Indian Literature*, 252. (July-August 2009)

5. Firaq as a Critic

Much ink has been expended over the artistic felicity and aesthetic acuteness of Raghupati Sahay Firaq Gorakhpuri (1896–1982) – one of the most admired poets of the subcontinent, who was also instrumental in transforming Urdu love poetry into a repository receptacle of multi-layered human consciousness that transcends the time and space barrier. Surprisingly, his wide-ranging, wholesome, discerning and equally forceful prose, containing a meticulous and candid, critical insight has hardly been subjected to dispassionate and assiduous evaluation.

Seldom do Urdu scholars and critics focus on Firaq's perceptive and sharp-witted criticism, which he practiced for almost three decades. There is no denying the fact that some Urdu critics have cursorily referred to his three books *Andaze* (1959), *Urdu Ki Eshqia Shairi* (1945) and *Urdu Ghazal Goiee* (1955) but they peremptorily describe him as the impressionistic critic, whose critical evaluation is based on interpreting the text in the backdrop of human emotions and impressions and who concentrates on conveying initial and stock responses which a piece of art may evoke. He takes pride in recreating the experience of the author, in the minds of the readers.

The onus of propagating such a mistaken notion rests with Firaq himself, who, on several occasions, including in the preface to 'Andaze', showed his penchant for impressionistic and aesthetic criticism. Firaq disagrees with the widely-accepted literary assumption that the spontaneous appreciation of poetry or the acclamation that a poet gets at any poetic symposium falls well short of criticism and most of the time, this sort of quick assessment proves to be misleading and erroneous.

For him, even casually discussed points pertaining to literature and poetry turn out to be quite apt and exact. He also makes it clear that he proffers a detailed discussion, covering aesthetic, intuitive and involuntary reactions, which a piece of art may stir up. He calls this sort of criticism, enormously popular in Urdu, creative criticism or living criticism. This sort of criticism is certainly more than what impressionistic criticism can do, in that it makes the text more tangible to the readers.

Firaq's self-proclaimed predilection for impressionism has prompted many critics not to concentrate on his writings thoroughly and they summarily describe him as a traditional critic who hardly discusses anything beyond the theme. It is pointed out that Firaq's writings owe much to a certain romantic vigour as he is a critic who recollects an aesthetic experience by taking recourse to amorphous and generalised critical terms. Further, Firaq's writings are described as somewhat pointless and trifling studies. Some critics do compare Firaq with Walter Pater and Oscar Wilde and it is also pointed out that the name of his book 'Andaze' is derived from Walter Pater's famous book *Appreciation*.

Some opine that Firaq's writings just convey impressions as his criticism revolves around narrating the relations between the poet and himself. It is also said that his style is completely bereft of exactness, clarity and comprehensiveness as too many adjectives are used, which create a miasma of fleeting impressions.

Casting the above-mentioned critical evaluation aside, if Firaq's prose is sifted, it will become unmistakably clear that these opinions convey a clouded vision which visibly falters on factual grounds. In order to acquaint the reader with the surface and deeper structure of a piece of art, Firaq, unlike his contemporaries, hardly concentrates on revealing the author's motive or analyses the text in terms of its relation to biography, historical contents, class discrimination, politics and myths. He focusses his attention on highlighting the intrinsic literary qualities of a text. He tries to turn attention to all possible questions that may crop up in one's mind while reading the text.

Considering the text as a verbal icon and a linguistic construct, Firaq studiously lays the foundation for a new model of criticism, unheard of in Urdu criticism which is prone to avoiding theory. His model seems to be eclectic, that draws its sustenance from almost every known model of criticism, including the Descriptive, Legislative, Historical, Romantic, Archetypal, Marxist, Formalist, and Structuralist ones.

He has broken new ground in Urdu criticism by introducing the eclectic or syncretic model which spurns any presupposed standard of assessing a work and explores all the possibilities of the text, by taking recourse to a synthesis of the theoretical frameworks and critical appraisal methodologies, pursued by a host of well-established literary theories. For Firaq, the text is basically an experience which ought to be delineated by analysing multi-sensory images that enable the reader to rediscover his sensibilities while reading the text, which also helps keep in check his own susceptibilities, and they also appear quite regularly in the text. He believes that the primary concern of criticism is to rediscover the experience of the writer.

Delineating the primary purpose of criticism, Firaq categorically declares:

> Criticism is not aimed at making opinions known and discussing points relating to external values of art and language. Critic must try to unveil the mystery of the writer's intuitive consciousness. He should make it a point to proffer a discussion on wisdom and feelings.
>
> (Gorakhpuri, 1959)

Firaq turned to criticism in the 1940s and prior to this, new criticism had found its way into literature. The term, 'new criticism' was first used in 1910 and with the publication of 'The New Criticism' in 1940, it gained prominence. The New Criticism's focus on leaving the personality of the author and historical perspective aside engendered the need to recognise the text as a self-contained unit, ie. a monad. Firaq seeks to analyze verbal complexities through which the completion of syntax or sense is deliberately differed until the end. Turning attention to various couplets of prominent Urdu poets such as Mushafi, Sauda, Zauq and Hali, Firaq aptly interprets the pattern in which words, compound verbs and various tropes are used to convey the meaning. Being well acquainted with the latest trends of critical theories that were then gaining currency in the west, Firaq took pains in analysing the creative usage of the word.

Analysing both the surface and the deeper structure of the art form by focussing attention on ambiguity, images, metaphor, metonymy, pun, homonym, rhyme, end rhyme, aporia, anagram, paradox, and other rhetorical devices, rather than paraphrasing the apparent theme, Firaq infused a new perspective into opinion-centred criticism. For the first time in Urdu, some specific inherent characteristics of the Ghazal were made the focal point in the discussion. New critics scorned the idea that the poet should have unflinching commitment to the external reality and Firaq was the first Urdu critic who initiated a lively debate on the issue of the commitment of a poet to any particular ideology.

Turning his attention to Tagore's poetry, Firaq aptly observed that Tagore was not committed to a particular ideology and his poetry unfailingly betrays a strong sense of poetic alienation. This is the cardinal principle on which the whole edifice of new criticism is built and Firaq meticulously used it as the defining tool of criticism. Firaq observes:

> Unlike scores of poets, Tagore did not subscribe to any religious belief, philosophy or political ideology. He never took oath in the session of logic or philosophy or religion. Many poets could not write without setting forth a principle. Even Shakespeare could not come out from the prison of his personality though he was a dramatist. He would narrate his autobiography through his heroes and heroines but Tagore's poetry is an exquisite illustration of the dramatic art and it is also a splendid example of poetic alienation.
>
> (Gorakhpuri, 1968)

Firaq's critical method reminds us of a prominent English critic, George Sainsbury as Firaq refers to his epoch-making *A History of English Prose Rhythm* (1912) time and again in his momentous monograph 'Urdu Ghazal Goiee'. Lesser known poets always fascinate Firaq and his studies on such poets not only aim at suggesting possibilities in reading their texts but also provide us with a candid and dispassionate appraisal.

Discussing rhyme and post-rhyme/end rhyme pattern of eminent Urdu poet Mushafi, Firaq points out that Mushafi quite often selects *Rah Gaye Ya Rah Gaya* as his end rhymes, in order to infuse a tantalising, resonating effect in the readers. He is the first Urdu poet who deliberately conjures up the image of inconclusiveness.

Highlighting the aesthetic sensibility of Mushafi, Firaq aptly remarks:

> No Urdu poet had used the word 'colour' as many times as Mushafi did and he used this image judiciously. Hence one could aptly describe Mushafi as a poet of five senses.
>
> (Gorakhpuri, 1959)

The study of creative usage of word, metaphor and images sums up the critical model of new criticism. Firaq's article on Mushafi is an illustration of this sort of criticism in Urdu. Never before has a critic pointed out that Mushafi used the motif of colour so vividly and tellingly. Firaq described his poetry as a picture gallery. According to him, Mushafi has a penchant for stirring up sight, hearing, taste, smell and touch simultaneously, which places him above his better-known Urdu poets of the nineteenth century. Mushafi's poetry, more or less consigned to oblivion, got its significance recognized with the publication of Firaq's well-researched article.

Firaq also initiates a detailed discussion on phonetic impact or words and sounds in his article on Hali, better known as the biographer and interpreter of Ghalib. He alludes to distinctive sounds used by him and points out that Hali's several ghazals end with vowel sound and his end rhyme scheme revolves around vowels. Hali has a distinct fascination for vowels, semi vowels and flapped, plosive, nasal and fricative sounds. Firaq asserts that:

> Hali used phonemes for evoking irony and ensuring the free flow of expressions. Rhymes finishing with 'alif' and the end rhymes based on 'Aik, Aik' (One by One) enable Hali to express his thoughts with

> felicity. Silent irony, flow of couplets – all these qualities are worth seeing. Hali has a distinct fascination for vowel sounds.
>
> (Gorakhpuri, 1959: 276)

Quoting hemistiches (a single line from a couplet) of Meer Anees 'Talwar Pe Talwar Chamakti Nazar Aae', 'Har Aankh Ko Pareeyon Ka Akhara Nazar Aae' and 'Tha Motiyon Se Dadman-e-Sahera Bhara Hua', Firaq points out that the phonetic impact of these hemistiches resembles the beat of a drum and that provides Anees's poetry with an admirable reverberating sound. (Gorakhpuri, 1959: 176)

Unlike the western educated contemporaries, Firaq was wary of applying the western principles of evaluating literature injudiciously and he makes it candidly clear:

> I do not reckon that Urdu literature or poetry and the eastern literature and poetry could be assessed by employing the critical principles that are used to evaluate the western poetry.
>
> (Gorakhpuri, 1959: 13)

It makes it clear that Firaq rejects the very notion of universal principles of criticism. It is worth mentioning that at one time, modernism propagated universalism vociferously. Rationalism and universalism were the grand narratives of modernity and Firaq was not swayed by the popular, predominant ideology of his time.

As we are aware, homosexuality is no longer perceived as unnatural or an aberration, by the post-modern society. Firaq, in his meticulous book on Urdu love poetry, described it as a revolt against the prevalent social norms:

> I ponder over the puzzle of homosexuality and the love between same sex for many years and I now endorse the view of Edward Carpenter that homosexuality is a revolt against the society that does not period attributes to be nurtured in females as a result she could not become a true companion of men. Similarly women seeking company of a woman, looks for attributes that are to be found in men.
>
> (Narang and Gorakhpuri, 2008)

These excerpts underscore the point that Firaq, unlike impressionist and romantic critics, does not confine himself to analysing the text in passing and generalised terms; conversely, he opts for a close reading of the text. He discusses morphology, semantics, syntax and phonemes, with a view to setting off the distinctiveness of the author. Firaq studies the text as an object and its structure always fires his imagination. It is far from the truth that Firaq tries to decipher metaphor with the help of another metaphor or he thinks that appreciation is more important than the critical evaluation.

In line with legislative criticism, Firaq suggests certain corrections and modifications while focusing on a text. His writings, bordering on suggestions, are geared towards keeping readers and the authors abreast of certain imperfections and blemishes. Legislative criticism always makes the author the focal point instead of the text.

In 'Urdu Ghazal Goiee' Firaq sometimes assumes the role of a nit-picker. Close on the heels of some prominent descriptive critics such as Dryden and Johnson, Firaq has shown his penchant for applying this theory. In interpreting couplets, he takes the reader's interest into account and makes him aware of both the exquisiteness and blemishes at once, by going into tropes, similes, images and symbols, having pored over several couplets. Firaq makes mentions of myth or prototype which alludes to the original tale from which innumerable tales are developed. For example Adam's departure from heaven is the prototype of separation and is essentially a critical method of archetypal critics.

In his momentous monograph on 'Urdu Ghazal Goiee', Firaq not only elaborates on themes but also lays open its conventional pattern. According to him, the sound and sense rhythm of a Ghazal makes it a microcosm within a macrocosm. In the Ghazal, the vowel sound, consonant sounds, aporia, anagram, homonym, pun, metonymy and metaphor of substitution, all come into play and make it a living organism.

Besides 'Andaze' and 'Urdu Ghazal Goiee', Firaq also wrote a veritable encyclopedia on love poetry, in Urdu. Being fully conversant with the western metaphysics and tradition, Firaq rightly mentioned that the work of art is not a creation of an individual only, as it owes much to tradition and experience which repeats itself frequently. He also takes recourse to the debate pertaining to culture and the social structure.

Contrary to the widely held view that Firaq is an impressionistic critic, a close look at his writings clearly places him among the exponents of syncretic criticism. It is also true that sometimes exactness eludes his critical writings and some of his favourite critical terms are hazy and indeterminate. But Firaq cannot be termed as the impressionist critic in that he ponders over the literary concepts with remarkable thoroughness and transmission of impression is not his basic concern.

Firaq's critical writings are highly readable and still are read by scholars and by ordinary readers.

Some of his evaluative statements have become very famous, for example, 'Mushafi is a poet of senses', or 'Ghazal is a series of climaxes' and the like.

It will not be an exaggeration to conclude that Firaq is the first Urdu critic whose point of view is eclectic. Prof. G. C. Narang aptly remarks, "Firaq rediscovered many classical poets and his book on Urdu love poetry is a classic." (Narang and Gorakhpuri, 2008)

References

Gorakhpuri, Firaq (1959). *Andaze*. Allahabad: Idara-e-Anees Urdu.

Gorakhpuri, Firaq (1968). *Hashiye*, Allahabad: Sangam Publication House.

Narang, Gopichand and Firaq Gorakhpuri (eds.) (2008) *Urdu Ki Eshqia Shairi*. Allahabad: Sangam Publication House. Sahitya Akademi

6. Ghalib Criticism

An Overview

No Urdu poet can vie with Mirza Asadullah Khan Ghalib (1797-1869) in terms of a dispassionate but uncontrived portrayal of the incongruities of human life. With a researcher's tenacity, he unwittingly transforms a myriad of experiences – sensuous, emotive, mystical and intellectual – into a unified pattern of unfading experience. His poetic method is clearly braced for converting the vagaries of daily life into excellent poetic material, interspersed with unsurpassable wit, and it leaves the literary critics and the common reader awe-struck.

In 1809, when Ghalib was only 12, his poignant poetry came in for a consummate discussion in *Takizra Umda-e-Muntakhiba*. Having praised the merits of the promising poet, Meer Mohammad Khan Suroor, the annalist, compared Ghalib with Mirza Abdul Qadir Bedil, one of the great exponents of the Ghazal. According to him, Ghalib effectively emulates the poetic diction of Bedil. Suroor's early adulation proved to be a straw in the wind as much ink has been expended over Ghalib's sterling contribution to the Urdu Ghazal in particular and other literary genres in general. Since the publication of his Urdu 'Deewan', hardly can any critic resist the temptation of focussing on Ghalib, no matter how plausible or non-perceptive his interpretation might be.

Ghalib's worldview and his matchless style, coupled with frequent use of paradoxes and witty comparisons or conceits has fired the imagination of innumerable critics and interpreters. Besides Urdu, a plethora of books, including full length translations of and commentaries on Ghalib's works, have been published in English, French, German, Russian, Persian, Arabic, Hindi and other Indian languages. A close look at all the Ghalib-related criticism reveals that his creative sensibility has not only drawn reasoned criticism but it has also provoked strong reactions. Further, it has also resulted in multiplicity of interpretations and commentaries that made him enormously popular.

The prodigious output of Ghalib has prompted the scholars, annalists and critics to focus their attention on his creative output. The literary annals, including 'Gulshan-e-Bekhar', 'Guldasta-e-Nazninan', 'Gulistan-e-Sukhan' and 'Tazkira-e-Ghoasiya', discuss his poetry, though the appraisal tends to be hyperbolic and lackadaisical. They give a nonchalant view of the splendour of Ghalib and that too in indeterminate, critical terms.

The above mentioned literary annals apart, the first detailed analysis of Ghalib's poetry and personality appeared in 'Aab-i-Hayat', the first ever history of Urdu language and literature. In his epoch-making work, 'Aab-i-Hayat', Maulana Mohammad Husain Azad, the most accomplished prose stylist of Urdu, dwells upon the distinctive features of Ghalib's poetry. For him, Ghalib's subtlety of expression, variation in themes, exquisite rendering of visual images, frequent use of stimulating metaphors, conceit and satirical quips make him one of the greatest exponents of the Urdu Ghazal. Ghalib's laudation aside, Azad essentially sings praises of Sheikh Ibrahim Baksh Zauq, a contemporary of Ghalib and the court poet. Azad has also come in for scathing criticism for his over-drawn and fulsome praise of Zauq.

The intrinsic appreciation of Ghalib's discerning poetry got the much needed fillip with the publication of Khawaja Altaf Husain Hali's *Yadgar-e-Ghalib* (1896). The book not only aims at acquainting the readers with the biographical details of Ghalib but also draws attention to the enormous wealth of imagery, metaphors, the lucidity of expression, prosodic variations like variations in metre, stress intonation, rhythm and rhyme, the scepticism about the nature of human psyche that he felt and at times, the abstract themes chosen by Ghalib.

Altaf Husain Hali's monumental work contributed immensely to the wide-spread popularity of Ghalib. Reading Ghalib's texts closely, Hali takes pains to make the readers realise that Ghalib's greatness lies in his amazing range of themes and he is the only poet whose tone is completely devoid of Melancholia. According to him, Ghalib is alive to the vigour and verve of Persian diction and imagery. He uses wit as a subtle and a most fascinating vehicle for the expression of his inner experience and his relation to the outer world.

Hali is at his analytical best while identifying those couplets and hemistiches, or single lines of the couplets of Ghalib which are considered allusive and deceptive. He also elucidates Ghalib's indirect, discursive mode of expression as a poetic method and asserts that Ghalib's poetry exudes a new layer of meaning whenever it is read. Hali sums it up by saying that the all-round fecundity of poetry came to a halt with the death of Ghalib.

Some critics point out that Hali interprets Ghalib by employing the eastern poetics only while Ghalib cannot be appreciated if the western poetics and aesthetic principles are not adhered to. Hali's observation that new critical idioms and canons are required to evaluate Ghalib's poetry bears testimony to his profound critical insight but he falters when he tries to evaluate the poetry, based on the clarity of its meaning. Along with a perceptive but susceptible appraisal of Ghalib's poetry, Hali does provide a candid and authentic account of Ghalib's life and times. It is perhaps beside the main point to draw a parallel between Hali and James Boswell, though a lot of Urdu critics have attempted it.

Hali is the first critic who focusses on Ghalib's prose and says that his ostensibly casually written letters betray a new kind of felicitousness. Ghalib's unparalleled creative dexterity and his quest for a new poetic idiom would have hardly come to the fore, had not Hali perceptively delineated its distinctive features. Ghalib's Persian poetry and his significant contribution to the growth of other literary genres also come in for a lively debate in *Yadgar-e-Ghalib* (Commemorating Ghalib).

Hali's momentous book went a long way in giving currency to Ghalib's moving and highly suggestive poetry. But Hali's unconditional acclaim did not deter Imdad Imam Asar from laying emphasis on some inherent imperfections in Ghalib, and he asserted that Ghalib's penchant for using the genitive case and trite metaphors, time and again, leaves the reader completely bewildered. Ghalib's propensity for using obscure Persian phrases and little known words makes it almost impossible to differentiate between Urdu and Persian.

In his two-volume book, *Kashiful Haqaiq,* Asar makes a strong plea for removing obscure and perplexing couplets of Ghalib but in the same vein, the author praises Ghalib for investing his couplets with many possibilities of meaning for the same couplet, which surface only on re-reading. According to him, Ghalib skilfully takes advantage of pre-existing themes by reclaiming them.

It goes without saying that serious attention was paid to Ghalib only after the publication of *Yadgar-e-Ghalib* and taking a cue from Hali, Abdur Rehman Bijnori used his thorough grounding in western education and wrote a book, *Mohasin-e-Kalam-e-Ghalib.* In his florid and over-ornamented prose, Bijnori heaps praise on Ghalib for the novelty of expression, poignancy of emotions and mellifluence, but his appreciation of Ghalib's poetry hardly draws its sustenance from a cogent literary theory. Bijnori's writing owes much to romantic and impressionist vigour as he tries to recreate the aesthetic experience of the poet. His analysis is completely bereft of exactness in that there are too many adjectives used and his book seems to be highly pretentious and unresponsive to the literary canons of evaluating poetry.

Casting Ghalib's fulsome laudation aside, Dr. Abdul Latif critically looks at his poetry in his English book *Ghalib.* He finds Ghalib's poetry quite messy and disorganised. According to him, his poetry seems completely devoid of self-realisation. In his nit-picking spree, Dr. Latif points out that Ghalib takes pride in regurgitating the themes of some well known Persian poets and asserts that Ghalib's poetry lacks innovation and individuality. In order to pin

Ghalib down, he compares Ghalib with Shakespeare and some other western poets and asserts that Ghalib lacks aesthetic vigour.

Ghalib's engaging poetry also impelled Maulana Abdul Salam Nadvi to initiate a detailed discussion. In his widely acclaimed literary history 'Shairul Hind', he asserts that Ghalib had greatly enriched the language by translating many terse Persian phrases and compound verbs into Urdu and he meticulously expanded the vocabulary, diction and the linguistic superstructure of the language. Ghalib's poetry denotes a high consciousness interspersed with a judicious blend of Persian phraseology. Ghalib's unparalleled creativity sometimes makes his couplets quite suggestive. Intricacy and obscurity contribute significantly to his poetic compositions. Under Ghalib's influence, stress was placed on new metaphors and similes and a resorting to wit became popular, he concludes.

As stated earlier, Ghalib's popularity has provoked strong and violent reactions. Mirza Yaas Yagana Changezi's book *Ghalib Shikan* bears an eloquent testimony to the fact. As its title suggests, the book is aimed at paring Ghalib down. Yagana himself proclaimed that his book came into being because some so called devotees of Ghalib who could hardly appreciate the aesthetic or literary merits, had unleashed a propaganda that was intended to belittle every other Urdu poet.

According to Yagana, Ghalib draws quite liberally from well known Persian poets and these borrowed ideas are lost in the labyrinth of his hackneyed style. Clumsiness of expression mars his poetry and to describe his poetry as original, simply amounts to literary betrayal. Yagana complains that Ghalib's poetry is dross and dreary and he flinches at some of the philosophical points elaborated by Mirza Bedil and Saeib.

Yagana's berating and tongue lashing by and large went unnoticed and Ram Babu Saxena, whose English book *Tareekh-e-Urdu Adab* was published just after 'Ghalib Shikan' bestowed acclaim on Ghalib. By dividing his poetry into two broad categories, Saxena holds that Ghalib's early poetry is marked with judicious use of Persian compound words and subtlety of expression. His later poetry owes much to sublimity and craftsmanship. Ghalib's poetry as a whole reflects his humanitarian mysticism and astonishing fluency in using evocative language and fresh imagery. The author also adores Ghalib's liberalism. According to him, Ghalib is an avowed enemy of religious narrow-mindedness and dogmatic approach.

In 1929, Mirza Mohammad Askari, who rendered Ram Babu Saxena's history into Urdu, brought out *Adabi Khutoot-e-Ghalib*. The book comprises Ghalib's letters that address literary issues and also throw light on how Ghalib goes about explaining his couplets. In his extended prologue, Mirza Askari aptly delineates the salient features of Ghalib's letters. Askari points out that Ghalib rests his letters on speech pattern rather than relying on the written word. He makes it a point to use comprehensible words, and stretched metaphors and obscure words are kept at bay. Ghalib strives to stamp out florid, over-ornamented and rhymed prose. Askari's work remains expository as he does not connect the statements of Ghalib with his creative output.

Ghalib's biography and his poetic method are extensively discussed in Sheikh Mohammad Ikram's book *Ghalib Nama* that was published in 1936. Sheikh Mohammad Ikram, with his thorough grounding in western thought, supplemented what was left out by Hali. Ikram's focus on reconstructing biographical details with graphic account throws new light on Ghalib's personality and his times. Ghalib's religion, world view, contemporaries, manners and habits are meticulously discussed.

He points out that Ghalib frequently takes recourse to anger, envy and other base emotions. At times, he hurls such harsh and rasping comments at his opponents which cannot be repeated. Ghalib's verbal onslaught against Persian lexicographer, Moulvi Mohammad Husain Tabrezi unfailingly affirms it. Sheikh Ikram drew up the complete chronology of Ghalib's 'Deewan'. It went a long way in explaining the formative stages of Ghalib, as a poet.

Malik Ram's book *Zikr-e-Ghalib* presents an exhaustive and truthful life sketch of Ghalib. Having tapped some relevant new sources,

Malik Ram provides a historical perspective to understand Ghalib and that too in a precise manner.

In 1936, Marxism made its way into Urdu with the formation of the Progressive Writers' Association. Critics owing allegiance to the Marxist ideology turned to Ghalib to receive authentication that his social commitment and awareness went on to contribute immensely to his greatness. According to them, Ghalib's poetry primarily drew its sustenance from social energies.

Majnoo Gorakhpuri, a prominent Marxist critic wrote *Ghalib: Shakhs aur Shair* in which social forces that shaped Ghalib's world view were discussed at length. He does recreate the academic and social atmosphere but he hardly connects Ghalib's poetry with the eastern poetics or western literary theories. Both the theoretical and syntactic levels of Ghalib's poetry escape his attention. The paraphrasing offered for some well known couplets of Ghalib is the only distinctive mark of the book and the author seems to shy away from going beyond the surface meaning and apparent social reality.

Another leading Marxist critic, Professor Mumtaz Husain published his book *Ghalib – Ek Mutala* which unmistakably shows the author's penchant for harping on economic determinants in which Ghalib was forced to live. Mumtaz Husain takes pains to highlight the social significance of Ghalib but he falters when he tries to place Ghalib in the Progressive perspective. Surprisingly, critical evaluation is absent all throughout this book as the author clumsily sputters out while explaining the couplets.

Ehtisham Hussain, who played a pivotal role in propelling Marxist criticism in Urdu, wrote a plethora of articles on Ghalib. In one of his widely acclaimed articles, 'Ghalib Ka Tafakkur', he connects Ghalib's poetical composition with dialectical materialism and traces its manifestations in Ghalib's poetry. The article running into forty one pages focusses attention on class struggle, class consciousness, capitalist economy, feudal system, rural economy and social exploitation.

Analysing some couplets of Ghalib that refer to some historical events, Hussain asserts that the couplets turn attention to historical realities which were pushing the then society towards certain disaster. Further, they manifest a lack of positive outlook. Ghalib was fed up with the prevalent sense of dejection and inertia. He could not sever his relation with the society but makes it abundantly clear that he had many things on his mind that he could not articulate unambiguously. The strong inherent current of solitude and alienation betrays his disgust. According to him, sycophancy and hypocrisy usually flourish in the feudal society which makes ambivalent behaviour popular and Ghalib denounces it vehemently.

Social conditions contributed immensely to the ever-growing popularity of Ghalib. He asserts that Ghalib's scepticism acquaints us with a new human consciousness and provides us with a perceptive insight into the essential nature of man.

Furthermore, a number of Marxist critics including Ali Sardar Jafri, Professor Mohammad Hasan, Qamar Raees, Dr. Zoya Ansari, Professor Mohammad Aqeel and Professor Sharib Rudaulvi etc. discretely make Ghalib the subject of a detailed study while essentially focussing their attention on his themes so that the social and cultural milieus can be fruitfully analysed in greater depth.

Professor Ale Ahmad Suroor, who dominated the literary scenario of the sub-continent for more than fifty years, wrote several articles on Ghalib. Professor Suroor, with his affected language and overwrought critical idiom, asserts that Ghalib put a premium on wit and his refulgent couplets exude meanings slowly. For him, Ghalib's uncluttered and colourful personality seeks refuge in religious and moral succour and goes along with human tower of strength.

Professor Gopi Chand Narang, in his widely acclaimed book, *Urdu Ghazal Aur Hindustani Zehan aur Tehzib* carefully delineates Ghalib's concept of love and points out that Ghalib had given sentimentalism, rationalism, spiritualism and materialism, equal importance. Ghalib's poetry betrays a natural human liking for love and love is not explained in spiritual terms only.

Professor Asloob Ahmad Ansari, whose thought-provoking studies are geared towards providing a candid and dispassionate appraisal, has written two books on Ghalib – *Naqsh-e-Ghalib* (1970) and *Naqsh Haye Ranga Rang*- in which the author has analysed the whole spectrum of the genius of Ghalib. With an even-handed concentration on both the content and the forms, Ghalib has been given the most extensive treatment through close and perceptive textual analysis. These books fill the gap in terms of textual analysis and that is demanding to be filled up.

Professor Asloob Ahmad Ansari, in a number of his articles, demystifies Ghalib and asserts that Ghalib is surprisingly closer to some romantic poets and the apparent similarity has prompted critics, who held romantic experience in high esteem, to describe Ghalib as the greatest poet of the Urdu language.

Ghalib's philosophical concepts came in for detailed discussion in *Fasl-e-Kalam-e-Ghalib* by Dr. Shaukat Subzwari and *Afkar-e-Ghalib* by Khaleefa Abdul Hakeem. Shaukat Subzwari makes it clear that Ghalib was not a philosopher but a philosophical poet as he dwells upon existence, extinction and continuance of life, through his couplets.

Wazeer Agha (*Ghalib Ka Zauq-e-Tamasha*), Saleem Ahmad (*Ghalib Kaun Hai*), Ralph Russel and Khurshidul Islam (*Ghalib: Life and Letters*), Faiyaz Mahmood (*Ghalib*), Ghulam Rasool Mehar (*Ghalib*), Dr. Yusuf Hussain Khan (*Ghalib Aur Ahnag-e-Ghalib*), Neyaz Fatehpuri (*Mushkilat-e-Ghalib*), Asar Lucknawi (*Mutala-e-Ghalib*), Aftab Ahmad Khan (*Ghalib – Ek Ashufta Nawa*) and others tried to focus on Ghalib and contributed significantly to the understanding of Ghalib.

In addition to books, some illuminating articles have provided the much needed breakthrough in Ghalib criticism. Such articles are 'Asloobiyat-e-Ghalib' (Gopichand Narang), 'Andaz-e-Guftugoo Kya Hai' (Shamsur Rahman Farooqi), 'Ghalib Aur Jadeed Zehan' (Dr. Wazir Agha), 'Ghalib Aur Asriyat' (Professor Alam Khoondmeri), 'Urdu Shairi Aur Ghalib – Ek Mutala' (Professor Akhtar Orenvi), 'Koi Batlao Ki Hum Batlayein Kya' (Professor Rasheed Ahmad

Siddiqui), 'Ghalib Aur Asr-e-Jadeed' (Professor Khalilur Rahman Azmi), 'Ghalib Mutaqid-e-Mir' (Dr. Syed Abdullah), 'Ghalib Bahaisiyat Muhaqqiq' (Prof. Qazi Abdul Wadood), 'Ghalib Jadeed Daur Mein' (Dr. Hamidi Kashmiri), 'Ghalib Ki Sheri Tarjeehat' (Professor Afzal Hussain), 'Ghalib Ka Lehja' (Prof. Abul Kalam Qasmi) and Qazi Jamal Husain's articles such as 'Ghalib Ki Nasr' and 'Kalam-e-Ghalib Mein Inhiraf Ki Suratein'.

Ghalib's Urdu 'Deewan' has attracted numerous perceptive interpretations. A veritable interpretation industry has come up on Ghalib's Ghazals. Shaukat Meeruti, a contemporary of Ghalib's, started it. He explores Ghalib with insight and at times, he discusses six or seven meanings of a couplet. In *Yadgar-e-Ghalib*, Hali provides plausible explanation of several couplets. Nazm Tabatabai, Hasrat Mohani, Abdul Bari Aasi, Nizami Badauni, Bekhud Mohani, Maulana Mumtaz Husain Suha, Professor Saleem Chishti, Josh Malsiani etc. made Ghalib's poetry an object of close textual studies. These commentaries are to provide a vivid and edifying explanation.

Shamsur Rahman Farooqui's *Tafheem-e-Ghalib* and Naiyer Masood's *Tabeer-e-Ghalib* are certainly improvements upon the above-mentioned commentaries as both are structured to wipe out the miasma of fallacy and misunderstanding plaguing Ghalib.

Shakilur Rahman's voluminous work *Mirza Ghalib Aur Hindi Jamaliyat* explains Ghalib's poetry in the Indo-Iranian aesthetic perspective. For him, Ghalib's moving visual images and fresh metaphors unfailingly manifest Indo-Iranian sensibility.

Ghalib criticism, notwithstanding its billowing size, makes it clear that the majority of critics and commentators mainly concentrate on themes of Ghalib. Their full-throated praise makes Ghalib a myth. There is no dearth of so-called Ghalib experts whose efforts revolve only around peripheral aspects of Ghalib and there are only a handful of books and articles that are insight-provoking, the rest being grossly inconsequential and trifling.

7. Literature, Culture and Social Consciousness

An Appraisal of Faiz's Prose Writings

Much light has been shed on the poetic dexterity and awe-inspiring aesthetic sensibility of Faiz (1911–1984) but his literary, cultural, aesthetic, artistic and social concerns, lucidly exposed to view in his prose writings, both in Urdu and English, have hardly been focussed on. Sheema Majeed's compilation of his *Culture and Identity, Selected English Writings of Faiz* (2005) and a few pieces on his Urdu prose (see also 'Faiz Ek Naser Nigar: Afkar Fair Number' by Saher Ansari, 'Faiz Ke Tanqueedi Ravaiyye' by Ali Ahmad Fatmil, 'Faiz Ahmad Faiz Bahaisiyat Naqqad' by Shafeeq Ahmad Ashrafi.) aside, seldom does one come across any discernable attempt to sift through the whole corpus of his prose writings, available in the form of a number of articles, reviews, laconic essays, prefaces, blurbs or short introductions to books, reviews, letters, speeches, discussions, radio talks, TV discussions, lectures and presidential remarks. These writings unfailingly prove that Faiz was certainly more than an aesthete who takes delight in conveying impressions in a florid style that a piece of art may evoke.

Most of his prose pieces are expository, evidently propelled along by the progressive canons of literature and many of them seem to have a pertinent point in them. The ideas get life in Faiz's tautly written prose and these pieces, embedded with fresh critical insights, establish his credentials as a sensitive critic. At times, his articles seem to make him a literary enthusiast whose writings are certainly more than the mere elucidation of pre-existent meaning.

Faiz' s prose was in no way inferior to his poetry, as many of his insightful articles, pertaining to literary theories, culture, painting, music, film, calligraphy, sculpture and architecture had appeared prior to publication of the first collection of his poems, 'Naqsh-e-Faryadi' in 1941.

As an erudite, clear-sighted and equally inquisitive critic, Faiz touched upon the theoretical and epistemological questions of literature time and again and his two Urdu books, *Meezan* and *Mate-e-Loh-o-Qalam* and the collection of his English writings, carrying more than two dozen theoretical articles, peel away accumulated layers of established truths. He proffers a critical and penetrating discussion on the theoretical contours of the literature in articles, such as 'Legacy of Literature', 'Literary Questions', 'Poetry and Sense', 'Writers, Where do you stand?', 'Thoughts on the Future of Ghazal', 'Concept of Beauty', 'Progressive Concept of Literature', 'Poet's Values', 'Literature and Democracy', 'Conceptual Poetry', 'Theme and Style', 'Literature and Culture', 'Expression and Representation', and 'Literature and Writer'.

Delineating the basic difference between expression and communication in poetry, Faiz asserts that if a poem does not take into account its readers and the poet pours forth his emotions to satisfy himself, it is expression but if the poet makes a deliberate effort to convey the same feelings to others, it is to be reckoned as an act of communication.

> The success of poetry is dependent upon communication, and expression cannot be successful if it fails to connect with others... If an artist turns the spotlight on an individual or invisible experience it is within an act of representation.
>
> (Faiz, 1973)

Focussing on the concept of beauty, Faiz equates beauty with harmony and asserts that beauty is not merely the negation of ugliness. He takes pains in analysing that which cannot be analysed:

> What then is beauty? It is both the tranquility of harmony and the turbulence of some other proportion. It is tangible as reality and as elusive as ghost, it is ecstasy, torment, experience and memory all rolled into an infinite variety, it acquires an emotional and

> perceptional permanence which age does not wither nor custom stale.
>
> (Majeed, 2005)

The term, 'infinite variety' seems to be an overstatement, as, here, Faiz unwittingly affirms the views of the romantic absolutists and one can hardly see any pretence of being an ardent admirer of the progressive literature; however, his unflinching loyalty to the Marxist aesthetic becomes quite evident.

In one of his well-argued articles, 'The Legacy of Literature', he argues that literature came into being when the first ray of consciousness enlightened the primitive man. Tracing the history of literature, Faiz remarks:

> The loneliness of the primitive man was replaced by close grasping in formalities which demand response and action. Thus the word looks on an additional function besides expression, namely communication. And then these communities discovered that the word was not merely a vehicle for expression of communication but could be bent to perform many other functions as well. It bound productive factors in communal labour by facilitating rhythmic movement. It was an instrument for increased knowledge through an exchange of observation of the material world.
>
> (Majeed, 2005: 149)

For Faiz, literature, by its very nature is a disguised chronicle of lived experience and cherished values of human life. Natural belief in humanism, peace, freedom and justice, a climate of feeling and sensitivity towards human suffering and pain and an articulate battle-cry against cruelty and oppression are things that constitute literature. Literature does draw its substance from day-to-day life and Faiz does provide an intense portrayal of little slices of life that constitute literature. His argumentative articles, 'Poetry and Sense' and 'Writers, Where do you stand?', seem tentative but they do attempt a few flourishes.

Going beyond poetic contrivance, Faiz, in his theoretical musing on literature, 'Writers, where do you stand?', urges fellow writers to raise their voices against all imperialist, racist and colonialist agencies so that the dream of universal freedom and universal peace could be realised. He calls for spelling out a new testament of creative effluence. One can easily conclude that Faiz, not infrequently, wears his Marxist learning lightly and the debate is habitually compromised.

Enumerating the inherent correlation between poetry and sense, the author describes language as the social product that builds up a healthy relationship between the individual and society, which also ensures the healthy growth of each. Citing the specific example of Tennyson's 'Lady of Shallot', Faiz says:

> The sense that poetry needs is not more (sic. mere) grammatical sense, but social sense. Why, after all, does The Lady of Shallot bore us? Because such a languid day-dream could only interest someone like The Lady of Shallot herself , a young lady in a convent , perhaps. We, with wars, revolutions, discoveries, famines, stalking around us, cannot possibly work up any interest in her. Poetry must be the most vivid expression of the most profound feelings of its age, forced into the channels of the most rigorous thought. Wordsworth told us long ago that a poet must be able to think as well as feel.
>
> (Majeed, 2005: 210)

The future of the most admired genre of Urdu literature, the Ghazal, is also eloquently delineated by Faiz. Notwithstanding its widespread adulation, the Ghazal has also been accused of providing an emotional solace to a populace, sick with loss and despair and that is why poetry was held responsible for the sack of Delhi and the moral decay and degeneration that plagued the Muslim society. It is a slur that is still alive in one form or the other and Faiz was seemingly piqued at it. Referring to the outcry led by Altaf Hussain Hali and Maulana Mohammad Hussain Azad, Faiz raises a very pertinent question:

> Why is it that whenever we are faced with a situation of social or political crisis or malaise, of all forms of writing the Ghazal is generally singled out as the prime target of criticism?
>
> (Majeed, 2005: 214)

Dishing out a tangible reply, Faiz describes the Ghazal as the most admired and, in fact the easiest genre that can be manipulated at will. Since the Ghazal transcends class barriers and symbolises the poetic personality of an age, it is held responsible for all the failings of this age. The Ghazal's unique communicability, combined with the novelty of metaphors and imagery and the choice of lilting metre and rhyme is invested with tremendous potential to enthrall people and Faiz rightly predicts that the Ghazal will continue to flourish because of its continual adjustability to the demands of aesthetic articulation of contemporary experience.

Explaining the salient features of the progressive literature, Faiz, in his Urdu article, 'Adab ka Tarraiqi Pasand Nazariya' described only those writings as progressive that may accelerate the pace of social development and that fulfil the artistic parameters. (Faiz, 1982)

Frequent use of hazy and ill-defined critical terms and bland paraphrasing of the theme was the hallmark of Urdu criticism, and unavailing interpretation, coupled with rhetorical flourish, left Faiz completely exasperated. In order to deflate airy-fairy critical terms frequently used by Urdu critics and reviewers, Faiz jotted down an expository article, 'Hamari Tanqeedi Istelehat'. At the outset, Faiz acknowledged the existence of critical idiom in Urdu but the vagueness and imprecision surrounding them paved the way for confutation and disorientation. He rightly points out that the ordinary words invariably falter on precision count but the literary terms need a high degree of accuracy. If they are not specified and focussed, they cannot be reckoned as literary terms.

For Faiz, many popular terms have become clichés as they no longer convey the specific meaning. Turning attention to some widely-used terms, Faiz begins by dispelling doubts about the simile and metaphor. For him, these rhetorical devices are just means not ends in themselves. By employing them, one can provide an appropriately amusing reading but any simile or metaphor is subservient to the intended meaning. Faiz clearly has a point when he asserts that no poet could survive if they put premium on these devices only. A simile for the sake of a simile or a metaphor for the sake of a metaphor does not augur well for the poetry and it is as misleading and fallacious as the concept of literature for the sake of literature. (Faiz, 1982: 42) Faiz rightly asserts that the meaning is always contingent and rational and it is essentially a network of cultural allusions and references.

Faiz also discussed simplicity, flow, spontaneity, wit, humour, pathos, poignancy, mysticism, quest for new meaning, figures of speeches, rhyme and sharpness of diction with admirable thoroughness and his arguments are backed by the perceptive analysis of the couplets of Ghalib and Iqbal.

Faiz also tears apart the argument that eastern literature ought to be evaluated by roping in eastern literary paradigms only. For him, this classification is superficial and equivocal as criticism in line with literature is directly linked to time and the social milieu. Romanticism, decadence, obscurantism and retrogression do not owe their existence to the west as they emerged as the natural outcome of our social development. Here the author clearly errs on the ground of historical thoroughness, as all the above mentioned literary trends flourished only in the western colonies.

'Values of Poetry', 'Literature and People', 'Conceptual Poetry', 'Creation and Imagination' and 'Theme and Style' are also his equally well-argued theoretical articles. Even in theoretical discourses and debates, Faiz does not forsake his unflinching commitment to aesthetic consciousness and he puts forward all his arguments logically. As a trained logician, he determines premises clearly and then refutes them by raising questions and every argument gets logically analysed.

Not infrequently, Faiz pondered on theoretical discourse and at times, he made thought provoking observations in his letters. New styles of expression hardly impressed him and he indicated his stand quite eloquently. In a letter to Akhtar Ansari Akbarabadi, Faiz observes:

> To develop a new style is not something one feels proud of. One may find new modes of expression attractive or disgusting but a new style that draws on theme and style of the past and present in equal measures and that stands out from the writings of the accomplished writers fascinates the sensitive reader.
>
> (Faiz, 1973: 196)

Sometimes Faiz's laconic remarks highlight a single moment of revelation. Poets and writers usually don't mind repeating themselves and Faiz tells them off: 'Imitating others is a serious flaw but emulating oneself is also a perilous lapse.' (Faiz, 1973: 201)

In another letter, he eloquently sums up poetry: 'Neither poetry rests on deftness nor relies on love. The essence of both is required only then it scales new heights.' (Faiz, 1973: 203)

Drawing a quaint analogy between imprisonment and the matters of the heart or affair de coeur, Faiz says that a painful uneasiness and sense of aloofness hold sway. Releasing the Urdu translation of Hooch Minh's poems, Faiz eloquently delineated the similarities and said that man shoves off secrecy, hypocrisy and longing for terrestrial things in affairs of the heart and so happen in confinement. (Faiz, 1973: 74)

In a radio talk, Faiz mocks at the view that Urdu poetry draws its sustenance from mysticism. Mysticism is not a lived or mental experience of Urdu poets; they just regurgitate Persian poets. Unfortunately there is no Urdu poet who can be mentioned as a genuine mystic poet as Iqbal too falters on this count. (Faiz, 1973: 244)

Faiz also makes some startling critical evaluation of some eminent Urdu poets. In his letter to Chirag Hasan Harat, Faiz informs him that recently he had read through Meer and Sauda again and it caused in him, a suspicion about Meer. He hesitates to believe that Sauda was greater than Meer. It is true that Sauda was no match for the awe-inspiring couplets of Meer but it is also a fact that the general level of Sauda's poetry overshadowed Meer and he was way ahead in craftsmanship. (Faiz, 1973: 203)

Besides perusing theoretical discourse closely, Faiz frequently deliberated on the texts of Khusro, Meer, Sauda, Mushafi, Ghalib, Zauq, Nazeer, Ratan Nath Sarshar, Abdul Haleem Sharar, Nazeer Ahmad, Munshi Premchand and Tolstoy. Analysing Ghalib's poetry astutely, Faiz says:

> Consumed by the agony of the remembrance
>
> The remembrance of night's festive company
>
> The one remaining candle flickers and dies
>
> So wrote Ghalib, the last and the greatest of the classical poets of the Urdu language. The image is characteristic. The flickering candle battling to the last breath, hopelessly and alone, against an inexorable end may well be the poet himself. He is the last articulate spectator of the glory that has departed - the colour and the gaiety, the warmth and good cheer, the 'Saqi of incandescent beauty', the 'singer of the ravishing voice' - and all else that peopled the emptiness of now deserted pleasure halls. Thus, in two symbolical lines the poet envisions the passing away of an age, a civilization and a way of life, his own nostalgia for happier times gone by, and an experience timeless and universal, in the life of all human individuals and human groups - the experience of the evanescence of time.
>
> (Majeed, 2005: 156)

Iqbal's concept of man fascinated Faiz and he discussed it in his four articles. For him, Iqbal speaks of man as a small atom of passion, set against the entire Universe. Man is great because he is the only creature to accept the challenge of creation. Man, the microcosm of pain, accepts the challenges of the stars and the moon and the sun and the universe. It is because of their greatness that the verse of Iqbal is elevated towards the end of his days, from beautiful to the sublime. (Majeed, 2005)

Apart from poetry, Faiz was also interested in fiction. He jotted down articles, 'Urdu Novel', 'Novels of Ratan Nath Sarshar', 'Sharar', 'Premchand' and 'Khadeeja Mastoor', in addition to writing short reviews on novels and short stories. Faiz's penetrating critical insight surfaces in these articles, time and again. His appraisals, though grounded in the progressive canon of literature, transcend time and space and make him quite close to the contemporary literary discourse. How does the text betray the intention of the authors? This is surprisingly answered by Faiz as early as in 1939.

Citing the example of Nazeer Ahmad's novels, Faiz says that his novels subvert his much touted reformist agenda and one can see a tantalising conflict between the Moulvi and the artist; usually, the artist emerges victorious. Nazeer Ahmad always wanted to harp on religious, moral or social issues but he would get lost in his characters. Despite spun out sermons, the villain of the novel turned out to be the hero. Nazeer Ahmad's famous novel, *Tabatun Noosuh*, clearly validates Faiz's assessment. The villain Kaleem, overshadows the hero. (Faiz, 1973: 160)

Premchand's portrayal of rural life did not impress Faiz at all and he was wary of calling Premchand a realist as he concentrated on highlighting the issues related to a particular class. Premchand's focus on sacrifice leaves Faiz completely baffled and for him, sacrifice no longer denotes bravery as it is quite close to cowardice. Many critics highly appreciated Premchand's effort at using rural language deftly but Faiz finds the use indistinct as one can find one sentence in rural dialect but the next sentence is written in chaste Urdu. According to Faiz, Premchand relentlessly pursued the platonic notion of love as seen in the two characters of *Chaugan-e-Hasti*; Sofia and Rona Singh's love is just childish. However, quite surprisingly, they are very mature in other affairs of life.

Concentrating on the texts of Ghalib and Iqbal, Faiz turns attention to the quest for identity in culture. For him, major cultural problems of underdeveloped countries are primarily social problems.

If Faiz's Urdu and English prose writings are simultaneously sifted through, one can see his critical acumen at its best and Faiz's growing acquaintance with new literary theories and shifting paradigms of culture and society become quite evident. Faiz is not an impressionist, as he ropes in different points with thoroughness. His writings denote that Faiz has very eclectic taste in literature.

References:

Ansari, Saher (1993) 'Faiz Ek Naser Nigar: Afkar Fair Number'. Karachi. April-May-June 1965.

Ashrafi, Shafeeq Ahmad. *Faiz Ahmad Faiz Bahaisiyat Naqqad*. Nusrat Publishers, Lucknow.

Faiz, Faiz Ahmad (1973) *Mata-e-Loh-o-Qalam*. Karachi: Danyal.

Faiz, Faiz Ahmad (1982) *Meezan*. Calcutta: West Bengal Urdu Academy.

Fatmil, Ali Ahmed. 'Faiz Ke Tanqueedi Ravaiyye'. *Aajkal*. February 2011. Delhi.

Majeed, Sheema (2005) *Culture and Identity: Selected English Writings of Faiz*. Karachi: Oxford University Press.

8. The Influence of Tagore on Urdu Literature

Urdu, spoken by more than 60 Millions (2001 Census), has usually been, though erroneously, perceived as a language that draws heavily from 'Erato' or sensual themes. Seldom does its power of strengthening cultural pluralism by macerating the creative output of a number of eminent writers, get applause from different quarters. Contrary to the widely held view that it regurgitates the themes of many well-known Persian and Arabic poets, Urdu literature, since its inception, keeps an eye on the authors who write in the languages spoken in different parts of India. In line with its age-long resilience, Urdu literature turns its attention to Tagore, whose unmatched creative insight and marked accuracy of sensibility is reflected in poetry, fiction, music, painting, acting and teaching, in equal measure. It goes without saying that the multifaceted personality of Tagore fired the imagination of those who have a panache for good literature.

Much before Tagore won the Nobel Prize, Munshi Premchand, who laid the foundation of fiction in Urdu, referred to him in his letters repeatedly and candidly, admitting that he had learnt the art of juxtaposing the mundane realities of life with eternal questions that constitute the mainstay of human existence, from Tagore. In a letter addressed to Munshi Daya Narain Nigam, dated September 10, 1910, he alludes to one of his unfinished stories that owed much to Tagore.

> I started writing a tale titled 'Vikramadat Ka Tegha'; I have jotted thirteen pages so far and intend to add five or six more pages. Finishing it quickly, I will send it to you. I have been ruminating over

> the story for many months. I believe I have emulated Rabindra's style successfully. It is not a bad imitation; the plot is entirely original.
>
> (Gopal, 1968: 39) [My translation]

In the same letter, Munshi Premchand advises the editor to obtain a painting of Tagore, as his journal no longer carries good colour photographs.

> *Zamana* (Era) has not been carrying a good colour photograph for the last two months. Ravi Verma's paintings are no longer in, why don't you contact Rabindranath Tagore as an exponent of painting.
>
> (Gopal, 1968: 41) [My translation]

Premchand's letters, written during the period 1910 to 1932, are replete with references to Tagore and his name appears twelve times. It looks pertinent to document these references, as it will certainly make it clear that Premchand was greatly influenced by the creative genius of Tagore.

As soon as *Geetanjali* won the Nobel Prize, a number of its translations appeared. In addition to *Geetanjali*, Tagore's other works were also rendered into Urdu. Imtiyaz Ali Taj was an accomplished playwright of Urdu who also ran a publishing house. Premchand, in his letter dated July 14, 1919, to Imtiyaz Ali Taj, enquires:

> 'Which of the works of Tagore will be published by you? July issue of *Zamana* (Era) will carry an interesting article on Tagore. It will invite your attention.' (Gopal, 1968: 82) [My translation]

Premchand wanted to know how many articles and creative pieces of Tagore appeared in the Modern Review and he sought the help of Munshi Dayal Narain Nigam, the editor of *Zamana* (Era) in his letter of September 27, 1919:

> 'How many articles and works of Rabindra Babu appeared in Modern Review? Later on all were published by Macmillan.' (Gopal, 1968: 88) [My translation]

Tagore's name again appears in another letter addressed to Daya Narain Nigam, dated January 3, 1921:

> 'Syed Abdul Majid's article goes well with (November) though it drew heavily from Rabindra Babu but it gives the impression of originality.' (Gopal, 1968: 133) [My translation]

Premchand's stories revolve around women who relentlessly toil for the betterment of family but their painstaking efforts, reformative in nature, hardly get recognition. 'Shroud' (Kafan) has the heroine, Budhiya who is a testament to the fact. Sympathetic portrayal of women apart, Premchand, quite surprisingly, denounces every manifestation of feminism in his letters and on that ground, he does not hesitate in despising Tagore's poems. Premchand's aversion towards feminism is revealed in a letter addressed to Imtiyaz Ali Taj. The letter dated September 14, 1920 says:

> 'I want to see literature as a masculine entity. I do not like feminism, no matter how it appears. This is the only reason I read many poems of Tagore with dislike. It is my natural failing and I cannot help it.' (Gopal, 1968: 116) [My translation]

Tagore got a rousing reception in Japan and it prompted Premchand to assert that Japan has not lost interest in the affairs of India. In his letter dated September 3, 1929 to Keshav Ram Sabherwal, Munshi Premchand observes:

> 'Tagore's grand reception in Japan has made it clear that it has not lost all its interest in India but it is regretted there were hardly any other examples of Japan's interest.' (Gopal, 1968: 187) [My translation]

Mentioning the names of the writers that left an indelible mark on him, Premchand writes to Banarsi Das Chaturvedi, a famous Hindi writer on June 3, 1930:

> 'I have not been influenced by any particular writer. I owed much to Pandit Ratan Nath Lucknawi and occasionally Doctor Rabindranath Tagore.' (Gopal, 1968: 203) [My translation]

Premchand held Tagore's writing in high esteem as he writes to Upendra Nath Ashk on March 23, 1932: 'Tagore's literary and philosophical articles are of high quality.' (Gopal, 1968: 237) [My translation]

Tagore is mentioned for the last time in his letter of August 10, 1932 and addressed to Jainendra Kumar, a famous Hindi writer: 'Recently *Shorshi* and other books of Tagore have appeared.' (Gopal, 1968: 241) [My translation]

In a letter addressed to Indernath Madan, Premchand explicitly disclosed that he consciously adopted the style of Tagore. In his letter of December 26, 1934, he mentions: 'Of course Tolstoy, Victor Hugo and Roman Ronald had left a mark on me. With regard to short stories Tagore irradiated my path at the beginning and later on I developed my style.' (Gopal, 1968: 332) [My translation]

In 1930, Premchand was invited to Shantiniketan but he could not make it as he got the invitation at the last minute. He explained the reason of not visiting Shantiniketan in his letter, dated March 18, 1836, to Banarsi Das Chaturvedi. (Gopal, 1968: 376) [My translation]

Since Premchand alluded to the texts of Tagore at least twelve times in his letters and he took pride in emulating the style of Tagore; one can easily conclude that Premchand, up to a certain extent, was influenced by Tagore.

Discussing the influence of Tagore on Premchand, a noted Marxist critic, Prof. Ehtisham Husain in his article 'Impact of Tagore on Urdu Literature', observes:

> Premchand's villages–innocent residents of the villages, distinct traits of their personality and his remarkable success in creating unified impression in the short structure of the story, all resemble with Tagore. There was hardly any significant tradition of short story prior to Premchand. It is quite possible that Premchand would have adopted purposeless romantic storywriting, had he not been acquainted with the vibrant characters of Tagore.
>
> (Husain, 1963) [My translation]

Delineating similarities between Tagore and Premchand, Abuzar Hashmi, a prominent Urdu critic, asserts: 'It is most likely that Premchand had learnt simplicity, lucidity of narration and depiction of reality, from Tagore. Premchand also rendered two novels of Tagore in Urdu.' (Hashmi, 2010) [My translation]

Some other critics and biographers of Tagore and Premchand point out that both tell stories with a strong sense of narrative. Taking a cue from Tagore, Premchand depicts the inherent weirdness of the upper caste with immense erudition. Both Tagore and Premchand have presented heartfelt accounts of the subaltern caught in the crossfire of the alien rule and repressive social customs. A number of characters depicting different points of view appear in their stories. Sometimes, thematic similarity between the two leaves the reader quite baffled. In his story 'Boraj', Tagore tells the story of a tehsildar of cotton tax while Premchand lays bare the hypocrisies and pettiness of Alopi Deen, in 'Namak Ka Darogha'. According to Mohd. Tahir Ali, Premchand's early stories are derived from the stories of Tagore. He even borrowed the plot of some stories from Tagore, and Tagore's story 'Master Moshaye' and Premchand's 'Captain' eloquently explain how Tagore influenced Premchand.

Besides Premchand, another prominent Urdu poet Josh Malihabadi, whose enthralling sensuous poetry coupled with revolutionary zeal, blazed a new trail in Urdu poetry, had a close affinity with Tagore as he spent six months in Shantiniketan at the invitation of Tagore. Josh provided a graphic account of his first encounter with Tagore and his subsequent stay at the institution for six months, in his widely acclaimed autobiography, *Yadon Ki Barat*. It is a terse and compelling account that provides great literary insights. It is a thrilling read that rarely gets caught in unnecessary flourishes. Josh's narration seems to be a perceptive analysis of the phenomenon called Rabindranath Tagore. With affection, admiration and adulation on the one hand and hostility on the other, Josh writes:

> When I returned to Lucknow from Ajmer, I found all round admiration for Tagore. I went there to meet him. Looking at me carefully he asked me in English, "Is it true that I am looking at the face of a young poet?" I replied with bowing head, "Probably, yes." He enquired about my name. I told my poetic name. Shaking hands with me, he said, "It was a pleasant surprise that Sarojini Naidu recited the translation of your poem 'The Dawn' yesterday and I saw you today. Your poem is unmatched and after listening to it I can describe you as the son of the dawn." After that, he told me that his father was a great scholar of Persian and the collection of Hafiz was found at his bedside. When I was leaving, he asked me, "Is it possible for you to stay at Shantiniketan with me for some time and explain the nuances of Hafiz's poetry so that I could acquaint myself with the spirit of his poetry?" I quite happily accepted his invitation. I reached there with my servant Jugnu and a number of

> books. Tagore gave me a rousing welcome and put me in the room of his student Burney.
>
> Life at Shantiniketan was very simple and the consumption of meat was prohibited. It did cause some sort of inconvenience but Jugnu would arrange 'meat' for me occasionally. Recreational morning bath at two times, morning and evening music and teaching under the shadow of thick trees, were an intrinsic part of Shantiniketan.
>
> ...though I was immersed in the radical thoughts rescinding mysticism, still Tagore's poetry greatly impressed me. The translations of his poetry would cast a spell on me. Occasionally I was still carried away by the mystical poetry. A poet can never be a prosaic and impolite philosopher. Had I been a Bengali I would have understood Tagore the way he ought to be understood. I deeply regret that I read his poetry with its English translations and that I could not understand him like Bengalis.
>
> (Ali, 2010) [My translation]

Turning his attention to Tagore's personality, Josh Malihabadi observes:

> Not being conversant in Bengali, I could not make a comprehensive assessment of his poetry as an authentic critic. Similarly, I could not give an absolute opinion about his personality.....And I spent six months with him, only six months, hence what could I say about him. The only thing I can say is that he is truly cosmopolitan, high spirited, extremely gentle, sensitive, unpretentious and an admirer of beauty.
>
> (Malihabadi, 2003) [My translation]

Josh's depiction reveals the virtuosity and variety of Tagore but he also turns attention to a trait of his that is at odds with the affable personality of Tagore. For Josh, the exhibitionist attitude of Tagore was repugnant.

> He was obsessed with a thing that left me completely annoyed. It was his penchant for publicity. It always filled me with a deep sense of dislike. Whenever a foreigner came for his interview, he would sit at a high-up place after getting himself fully spruced up. Ambergris would light up behind him. Fully surrounded by beautiful girls he would give the interview in such a manner that the interview seeker would get the impression that he was speaking to a divinity.
>
> (Malihabadi, 2003) [My translation]

This trenchant observation combines wit and sobriety and provides insights into the life of Tagore.

Professor Mohammad Hasan, Professor Ehtisham Husain, Professor M. Ziauddin and a number of other writers discussed the similarity between Tagore and Josh. The quest for beauty and love is the common strand that runs through the poetry of Tagore and Josh.

A noted Urdu scholar, Maulana Abdul Majid Daryabadi reviewed Josh's book *Rooh-e-Adab* (Spirit of the Literature) in 1921 and opined that Josh's prose rendering drew its sustenance from Tagore.

Not much has been written on how equally eminent contemporary poets Iqbal and Tagore influenced each other. Some scholars did draw an analogy between them. For Abuzar Hashmi, Iqbal's poetry exudes a close thematic affinity with Tagore's. Both Tagore and Iqbal seem to have been enamoured by the beauty of nature. Iqbal was an avowed enemy of lethargy and sloppiness that were rampant among Indians in the first half of the twentieth century and so was Tagore. They put premium on patriotism. Quoting a poem of Tagore titled 'Bolaka', Hashmi draws a parallel between the poetic motifs of the two great poets. Tagore's 'Rajhans' is akin to Iqbal's 'Shaheen'. Further, both show a deep concern for humanity. (Hashmi, 2010) [My translation]

Abuzar Hashmi definitely has a point in his comparison. It is also known that Tagore was fully aware of Iqbal and his poetry. Quoting Prabhat Kumar Mukhopadhyaya, Shanti Ranjan Bhattacharya in his Urdu book *Hayat-o-Khidmat* pointed out that Tagore visited Lahore in 1934 and he went to Iqbal's house but he was away from Lahore. Tagore appreciated Iqbal's poetry in his letter to Abbas Ali Khan Lama Hyderabadi. Praising Iqbal's creative genius, Tagore writes:

> Being not conversant with the languages in which Iqbal wrote I could not understand the depth of his creativity and I could hardly dare to express my opinion about his poetry. Iqbal's popularity prompts me

> to believe that his couplets are jewels that have the effulgence of the eternity of literature.
>
> (Bhattacharya, 1990) [My translation]

Tagore composed a poem on Iqbal when he died in 1936.

Another prominent scholar and accomplished prose writer, Maulana Abul Kalam whose euphuistic prose opened new vistas upon Urdu prose writers, was deeply influenced by the florid narration of Tagore. Maulana Azad saw him in 1936 and in his preface to the translation of *Geetanjali* by Abdul Aziz Khalid, he gives a gripping account of this brief meeting. According to Azad, he saw Tagore for the first time in 1936 when he was entering the Kalabhavan and was being assisted by Shri Anil Chand and Shri Nand Lal Bose. Tagore was on a wheelchair but his frail body seemed very vibrant and cheerful. Tagore would cast a long look at every painting and he was deeply moved by a painting. He said:

> I regret that hardly any time is left for me. I have to do a lot but I hardly see any opportunity. My hands have become useless, how could I find sensitivity of fingers. There is no flexibility left in my body, I have lost everything. If I get some more time, I will complete the works that are pending.
>
> (Khalid, 2010) [My translation]

In his journalistic and literary writings and even in his widely-acclaimed letters, Maulana Azad deliberately employed the ornate but equally perceptive style of Tagore.

Akbar Allahabadi, who employed wit, humour, irony and satire with remarkable creative dexterity and whose couplets are still recited time and again, was an admirer of Tagore. Niyaz Fatehpuri, who has the credit of translating *Geetanjali* in Urdu for the first time, narrates an interesting anecdote:

> One day I was sitting near Akbar Allahabadi with the English translation of *Geetanjali*. Looking at it Akbar said that if music was translated into poetry and it could express feelings, then it would take the shape of Tagore's poetry. The back cover of the translation carried the photograph of Tagore that prompted Akbar

> to observe: 'The painting of Khamaj (a kind of Ragini) is drawn very similar to it.'
>
> (Fatehpuri, 1914) [My translation]

The first translation of *Geetanjali* appeared in Urdu in 1914. Niyaz Fatehpuri, famous editor of the literary journal 'Nigar' rendered it into Urdu with the help of its English translation.

Geetanjali's florid narration fired the imagination of many Urdu poets and prose writers. *Geetanjali* was frequently rendered into Urdu and Abdul Aziz Khalid, Nirmal Chander and Syed Zaheer Abbas were the translators. Josh Malihabadi and Munawwar Lucknawi also rendered some poems of *Geetanjali* into Urdu. Professor M. Ziyauddin translated the poems of Tagore directly from Bangla and these are the only direct and authentic translations. Firaq Gorakhpuri translated one hundred and one poems of Tagore into Urdu and it was published by the Sahitya Akademi, Delhi. Majaz rendered 'Gardener' into Urdu and Malik Ram too translated it in 1944. Pustak Bhandar, Amritsar, published it. Many poets well versed in Urdu and Bengali translated Tagore's poetry. They are Parvez Shahidi, Salik Lucknawi, Ezaz Afzal, Qaiser Shameem, Ain Rasheed, Mushtaque Anjum and the like.

The translations of Tagore left an indelible mark on Urdu literature and it provided sustenance to two literary movements in Urdu. Romanticism in Urdu owed much to Tagore and it engendered a new genre 'Adab-e-Lateef'. Tagore directly influenced Sajjad Haider Yaldram, Iaam Ahmad Akbarabadi, Majnoo Gorakhpuri, Mehdi Afadi, Neyaz Fatehpuri, Mulla Ramozi and the like. Blank verse and prose poetry came into existence, owing to the influence of Tagore.

The Progressive Movement committed to the Marxist ideology was set in motion in 1936. The progressive writers ranted against romanticism and the over-emotional notion of love, and they looked up to the distinguished writers for guidance. Premchand and Tagore did not disappoint them and they expressed their solidarity with them. Premchand delivered the presidential address at its first conference and Tagore sent a message to the progressive writes for their Allahabad Conference held in 1937. In his message, Tagore asked the writers to get along with people if they want to understand them.

> They cannot do their work if they remain cut off from people as I did. Having ignored the masses for a long period, I committed a blunder. Now I realise it and that is why I exhort you not to emulate me. My conscience thinks longingly of humanity and society. If literature is not fully alive to human aspirations it will never attain any success.
>
> [My translation]

The concept of emancipation of human beings and an unflinching commitment to human concerns are the marked features of Tagore's poetry but Urdu poets perceived him as a poet who excels in creating a multitude of emotional effects. This erroneous but widely held view about Tagore prompted progressive poets to take a cue from Nazrul's revolutionary poetry.

Hamidullah Afsar and Parvez Shahidi, two famous progressive poets, roped in the falcon imagery of Tagore frequently in their poetry. Parvez Shahidi wrote a poem 'Imprisoned Songs' on the occasion of Tagore's birth centenary celebrations and Hamidullah Afsar translated 'Seeshu' into Urdu. For him, if one has the collection of Hafiz in one hand and *Geetanjali* in the other, then he is the most prosperous person.

Tagore's focus on subtlety of narration and interiority of experience did not go well with the writers committed to modern sensibility but Tagore's fiction continued to inspire fiction writers. Many novels, plays and short story collections of Tagore appeared in Urdu. *Gora* and 'Kabuli Wala' got wide spread currency in Urdu and a modern short story writer, Anwar Qamar created his short story titled 'Kabliwala Ki Wapsi', on Tagore's 'Kabuli Wala'. The story was written in the backdrop of the Soviet intervention in Afghanistan. His story begins where Tagore's hero completes his journey. It is perhaps the first example of creating fiction upon fiction, the hallmark of post-modern fiction.

Much ink has also been used on Tagore's biography and works; many literary journals such as 'Aajkal', 'Rooh-e-Adab', 'Naya Daur' and 'Maghribi Bengal' etc. brought out special issues on Tagore. Scores of books such as *Aalmi Shair Guru Dev Doctor Rabindranath Thakur Ki Jeevni* by M. Abdus Salam Zaki (1961), *Rabindranath Tagore* by Ehsan BA, *Tagore* by Nadim Seetapuri (1961), *Iqbal, Tagore and Nazrul* by Shanti Ranjan Bhattacharya and *Rabindranath Tagore: Hayat wa Khidmat* by Shanti Ranjan Bhattacharya, appeared in Urdu.

The above-mentioned details make it clear that Tagore's creative output has left an ineffaceable impact on Urdu literature and his creativity still seems to be a perennial source of inspiration.

References

Ali, Hafiz Mohammad Tahir. 'Tagore and Premchand as Short Story Writers'. *Maghribi Bengal, A Special Issue on Tagore* (May–July 2010) 142.

Bhattacharya, Shanti Ranjan (1990) *Rabindranath Tagore: Hayat-o-Khidmat*. Kolkata: West Bengal Urdu Academy.

Fatehpuri, Neyaz (1914) *Preface to Araz-e-Nagma* (Translation of Geetanjali), Delhi: Azad Book Depot.

Gopal, Madan (eds) (1968). *Premchand Ke Khutoot*. New Delhi: Maktaba Jamia.

Hashmi, Abuzar (2010). 'Aiwan-e-Urdu Mein Tagore Ki Bazgasht'. *Maghribi Bengal, A Special Issue on Rabindranath Tagore* (May–July 2010) 96.

Husain, Ehtisham. (1963) *Afkar-o-Masail*. Trans. Shafey Kidwai. Lucknow: Naseem Book Depot.

Khalid, Abdul Aziz. 'Preface to Gul-e-Nagma'. *Maghribi Bengal*, July 2010.

Maghribi Bengal, A Special Issue on Tagore (May–July 2010) 33.

Malihabadi, Josh (2003) *Yadon Ki Barat*. Delhi: Danish Publishing Company.

9. Early Journalistic Endeavours of Sir Syed Ahmad Khan

The first newspaper of India, *The Bengal Gazette* or *Calcutta General Advertiser* was launched in 1780, from Calcutta. An employee of the East India Company, James August Hickey was its founder; hence it was also known as *Hickey's Gazette*.

In India, Urdu and Persian journalism began almost concurrently. Raja Ram Mohan Roy launched a Persian newspaper, *Miratul Akhbar* from Calcutta in 1822. Tahir Masood points out that the *Miratul Akhbar* was not only the first Persian newspaper of India but also the first in the entire Persian speaking world, including Iran. (Masood, 2002)

A month earlier than that, the first Urdu newspaper, *Jam-e-Jahan Numa* was published from Calcutta. Its first issue hit the stands on 20 March, 1822. Harihar Dutt was its owner and Munshi Sukh Lal was its first editor.

About a decade later, *Delhi Urdu Akhbar* was launched from Delhi. The first newspaper from Delhi was launched in 1836. Sir Syed says that the *Urdu Akhbar* is believed to have made its appearance in 1836 in Delhi. (Krishnamurthy, 1966)

Urdu Akhbar was started by Moulvi Mohammad Baqar, a renowned scholar from Delhi. It was generally regarded as a complete newspaper that published informative and thought-provoking material on topics of public interest. *Urdu Akhbar* enjoyed enormous popularity.

Since his early age, Sir Syed (1817-1898) had been a regular reader of *Urdu Akhbar,* which fact he acknowledged time and again in his writings. Having developed a way with words since his childhood, he started trying his hand at various genres of literary and journalistic writings. Before writing substantial books on history, archaeology, mysticism, metaphysics, manners, etiquette and other subjects, Sir Syed got extensive hands-on journalistic training, under the pressure of a deadline, in one Urdu and one Persian newspaper.

Not much has been written about Sir Syed's early journalistic writings and his professional stint with the newspapers had almost escaped the attention of his biographers, including Colonel G.F.I. Graham (1875) and Altaf Husain Hali (1901). Even the focussed studies of his journalistic writings hardly refer to his early journalistic endeavours.

Here, an attempt is being made to focus on the newspapers that attracted Sir Syed initially and to show that he got himself associated with them in one capacity or the other.

(a) *Syedul Akhbar:*

The popularity and respectability of *Delhi Urdu Akhbar,* the first Urdu weekly of Delhi, had inspired Syed Mohammad Khan, elder brother of Sir Syed, to start a newspaper and he launched a weekly, *Syedul Akhbar* in 1837, which was erroneously described by Margarita Barns, as the first newspaper of Urdu. (Barns, 1940)

Nadig Krishnamurthy endorses her by asserting that *Syedul Akhbar* is generally mentioned as a pioneer in the field of journalism. (Krishnamurthy, 1966)

Margarita and Krishnamurthy's assertions aside, the year of *Syedul Akhbar*'s launch seems to be a debatable issue. Notwithstanding the controversy, it is generally believed that Sir Syed learnt his early professional lessons and got hands-on training while working for *Syedul Akhbar*. Since a lot is unclear about *Syedul Akhbar,* it looks essential to call attention to the claims and counter claims related to the exact year of its launch, dispassionately.

A number of historians of early Indian Journalism including P. R. Bhatnagar (1947), Imdad Sabri (1953), S. Natrajan (1955), Mohammad Ateeq Siddiqui (1957), Abdus Salam Khurshid (1963), Nadig Krishnamurthy (1966) and Emmet Davis (1983) have claimed that *Syedul Akhbar* was started in 1837. Conversely, a reference in an official report, published by the Government Press, had put a question mark on the year of its publication.

The Government of the North Western Provinces prepared an administrative report for the perusal of the Lieutenant Governor of the North Western Provinces. Mohammad Ateeq Siddiqui (1961) tracked down the report that gives a detailed account of the newspapers and publications of the North Western Provinces during the period of 1848 to 1853. Mr. A. Shakespeare, Assistant Secretary of the Government, had prepared the report for the year of 1848, which states that *Syedul Akhbar* was started in 1841 and the paper was said to be the organ of the Sunni sect of the Muslims and Syed Abdul Ghafoor is its owner and editor.

This prompted two historians of early Urdu Journalism, Nadir Ali Khan (1987) and Tahir Masood (2002) to conclude that the *Syedul Akhbar* was started in 1841, not in 1837 as claimed by Hali and the other historians of Urdu Journalism.

The report in question pertains to 1848 and it makes a casual reference to *Syedul Akhbar*. It mentions the name of its proprietor, Syed Abdul Ghafoor but authentic contemporary evidence makes it clear that its owner was Syed Mohammad Khan who had set up a lithographic Press in Delhi. The first collection of Ghalib was printed at this Press. The title page of the first edition of *Diwan-e-Ghalib* carries the following line at the bottom: 'Printed at Syed Mohammad Khan's lithographic press in the month of Shaban 1125 Hegira i.e. October 1841 under the supervision of Syed Abdul Ghafoor.' (Siddiqui, 1957)

It makes it clear that the press was owned by Syed Mohammad Khan and Abdul Ghafoor was an employee, but the report erroneously describes him as the owner. Further, one more contemporary evidence contradicts the official report convincingly. The news of

Syed Mohammad's death appeared in a newspaper of Bombay, that says: 'Syed Mohammad Khan, the owner of the *Syedul Akhbar* died following a bout of fever.' (Ahsanul, 1846)

The official report, used as definite proof by Ateeq Siddiqui (1966), Nadir Ali Khan (1987) and Tahir Masood (2002), did make a passing reference to the year of *Syedul Akhbar*'s launch after a gap of eleven years, without giving any concrete proof for the same.

A close associate of Sir Syed, Munshi Zakaullah who lived in Delhi, mentioned that *Syedul Akhbar* was launched in 1837. Hence the official report seems quite fallible, as another equally reliable contemporary evidence points out that *Syedul Akhbar* was launched in 1837, not in 1841. Needless to say, simple assertion cannot take precedence over the contemporary evidence.

Some historians of Urdu journalism assert that *Syedul Akhbar* was named after Sir Syed. It shows Syed Mohammad Khan's affection for his younger brother. This assertion has gained currency despite it being imprecise; Syed was the family surname and Ahmad was the real name of Sir Syed. Had it been Ahmadul Akhbar, we would have accepted the argument. Syed was also very much part of the editor's name – Syed Mohammad Khan. The title of the newspaper was based on family lineage – Syed.

The files of *Syedul Akhbar* have been lost in oblivion but the files of some contemporary newspapers such as *Sadarul Akhbar* (Agra) and *Ahsanul Akhbar* (Bombay) which reproduced the material from *Syedul Akhbar*, are available. One could collect some information from them; Tahir Masood quoted some news items of the *Syedul Akhbar* that reappeared in *Sadarul Akhbar*. (Masood, 2002)

Syedul Akhbar appeared on Wednesday and its subscription rate was fixed at two rupees, monthly. Its editor, Syed Abdul Ghafoor was well-versed in legal affairs as a number of editorials appeared on the bills and regulations enacted by the British Government. The newspaper was very popular among the advocates. (Siddiqui, 1957)

Since Syed Mohammad Khan was in the government service, he appointed Syed Abdul Ghafoor as the editor. He was a junior judicial officer, Munsif and at that time was posted at Hutgaon, Fatehpur District.

The circulation of *Syedul Akhbar* was, according to the official report, restricted to 50, in 1844. 11 copies were complimentary and 39 were dispatched to its subscribers with the following break up: Muslims 32, Hindus 6 and the Governor General 1. (Hali, 1979: 34)

Hali made a brief reference to *Syedul Akhbar* and claimed that Sir Syed got hands-on training at his elder brother's newspaper and also got his early articles published in it:

> He (Sir Syed) planned to develop the newspaper *Syedul Akhbar* which had been managed by his brother and published a book on the buildings of Delhi. Although the newspaper was nominally directed by someone else, it was in fact Sir Syed who contributed most of the articles.
>
> (1979: 35)

Endorsing Hali, Sir Abdul Qadir, a prominent Urdu writer, asserts that Sir Syed laid the firm foundation of his journalism by writing articles for *Syedul Akhbar*. (Qadir, 1957)

On the contrary, Tahir Masood, without marshalling any concrete evidence, asserts that Sir Syed sold the newspaper to Syed Abdul Ghafoor in 1848. This is the reason the administrative report of the North Western Provinces described Syed Abdul Ghafoor as the owner of the newspaper. (Masood, 2002) The author, however, does not have any concrete evidence to lend credibility to his claim.

One has no option but to rely on Hali and some other contemporary writers who talked about Sir Syed's association with *Syedul Akhbar*. As stated earlier, its files are lost, hence one could not say how many articles Sir Syed contributed and after the death of his elder brother, how he shaped and developed the newspaper.

Though Sir Syed's articles carried by *Syedul Akhbar* are not accessible, the official report of the North Western Provinces Government, for the year of 1848, does make a reference to the content of it. It says,

Syedul Akhbar devoted the first two pages to news. Its latest issue carried an article on the old building of Jaunpur on the front page.

The description of the content and display pattern of *Syedul Akhbar* is a testament to the fact that Sir Syed was instrumental in shaping it as he retained the same news display pattern when he started his multilingual weekly - *The Aligarh Institute Gazette* from Aligarh, in 1866. In the *Gazette* too, the first two pages usually carried news.

Similarly, Sir Syed's interest in archaeology, culture and history was well known and he wrote extensively on these topics. One could easily guess who wrote the article on the building of Jaunpur. Further, he published similar articles in the *Aligarh Institute Gazette,* later.

Though Sir Syed's stint with *Syedul Akhbar* is still not well documented, the material gathered from some contemporary newspapers and other sources pertaining to *Syedul Akhbar* did testify that Sir Syed had learnt the art of journalistic writing by working with *Syedul Akhbar*.

(b) *Zubdatul Akhbar*:

Sir Syed's stint with *Syedul Akhbar* was mentioned by Hali and other biographers of Sir Syed, but his association with a Persian newspaper was not mentioned in all of the extensive scholarly literature written on him. Further, no historian of early Urdu journalism, including Imdad Sabri, (1953), Mohammad Ateeq Siddiqui (1957), Abdus Salam Khurshid (1963), Nadir Ali Khan (1987) and Tahir Masood (2002) discusses his connection with *Zubdatul Akhbar*.

Zubdatul Akhbar, a prominent Persian newspaper of the North Western Province, was launched in 1833 from Agra. Nadig Krishna Murthy asserts:

> Between 1830 and 1840, a few Persian newspapers could be found. One of the first newspapers, Zubdatul Akhbar, was started in 1833 by Munshi Wajid Ali Khan in Persian language. He was the editor and proprietor, and he commanded respect for his tact and his ability. His paper was subsidized by five rulers and rich merchants with

> a view to guaranteeing that the newspaper did not publish matter likely to lower the donors in the public esteem.
>
> (Krishnamurthy, 1966)

J. Natrajan quotes the official report of the Government of the North Western Provinces, verbatim, without acknowledging it explicitly, while discussing *Zubdatul Akhbar* and its editor, Munshi Wajid Ali Khan. He writes:

> Wajid Ali Khan was a cautious editor rarely hazarding his own opinions or in any way laying him open to attack. Expression of dissatisfaction was rare and when indulged in clothed and flowery language. His sources were the English and other newspapers. Wajid Ali Khan did not favour the Europeanized way of life and his conservatism, subtly expressed, appealed to his circle of readers. His conservatism had found its target in the periodicals edited under the auspices of Government educational institutions such as *Sadarul Akhbar*, the Agra College newspaper.
>
> (Natrajan, 1955)

Zubdatul Akhbar, the first Persian newspaper of the North India, was a weekly that appeared on Fridays. The English newspapers were its main sources of news and other editorial content. It ran into four pages and its monthly subscription was one rupee. It had the distinction of being the largest circulated newspaper of North India.

Tahir Masood points out that the files of *Zubdatul Akhbar* are no longer available but some of its news stories were reproduced in *Asadul Akhbar*, Agra with proper attribution. It shows that the newspaper displayed a keen interest in scientific experiments and discoveries being made in the West. (Sabri, 1955: 72)

Abdus Salam Khurshid asserts that *Zubdatul Akhbar* was held in such high esteem that its excerpts appeared even in the English newspapers such as the *Bengal Harkaru* and the like, quite regularly. This was the unmatched distinction and no other Persian newspaper of that time had such a reputation. (Masood, 2002)

The official report prepared by the Government of the North Western Provinces informs that the editor of *Zubdatul Akhbar*,

Munshi Wajid Ali Khan, was a well-known Persian scholar. He wrote impeccable and melodious prose and the people subscribed to his newspaper for just that.

Munshi Wajid Ali Khan was a profound scholar of both Urdu and Persian and he wrote a book on Urdu grammar, *Guldasta-e-Anjuman*.

Imdad Sabri provides some important details about *Zubdatul Akhbar* and its famous editor, though he hardly turns attention to the content and display pattern of the newspaper. According to him, Munshi Wajid Ali Khan was the resident of Hoogli, Bengal and since his childhood, he had a flair for writing. At the age of 12, he left home and wandered the world around, before settling down in Agra. He spent considerable time in literary pursuits before launching the first Persian newspaper of the North-Western Province, *Zubdatul Akhbar*. He edited for almost two decades. He was a poet of both Urdu and Persian.

Zubdatul Akhbar was very popular when Sir Syed reached Agra. In Agra, Sir Syed used to read *Zubdatul Akhbar* with great interest and he visited the newspaper office quite often, to assist Munshi Wajid Ali Khan in the production of the newspaper.

Had the files of the *Aligarh Institute Gazette* (1866 to 1898) not been sifted, Sir Syed's association with *Zubdatul Akhbar* would not have come to the fore. Sir Syed did talk about his connection with the newspaper in a stand first – introductory remark that precedes an article or a report in a newspaper.

In 1878, Munshi Wajid Ali Khan, editor of *Zubdatul Akhbar*, wrote a strongly-worded piece against the *Aligarh Institute Gazette*. Showing remarkable poise, Sir Syed reproduced it in his newspaper with the following stand first.

Our Old Friend Munshi Wajid Ali Khan and We:

> We traveled outside Delhi and reached Akbarabad (Agra) probably in 1838. On reaching here, I started admiring respected Munshi Wajid Ali Khan. At that time *Zubdatul Akhbar* was being published from Agra and he was its editor. I frequently visited the newspaper

> office and learnt a lot there. We could not see him for long and believed that he might have forgotten me. But I am delighted to learn that he has not failed to think of me and expressed his views on our newspaper. I got an opportunity to assist him when I was at Agra; it was proved to be a highly rewarding experience.
>
> (*The Aligarh Institute Gazette,* 12 November 1878) [My translation]

It is an explicit acknowledgement of his association with *Zubdatul Akhbar*.

Sir Syed was very good at Persian and had already gotten hands-on training at *Syedul Akhbar*, Delhi. Therefore, he might have found it quite appropriate to lend a helping hand to Munshi Wajid Ali Khan. The issues of *Zubdatul Akhbar* are not available; hence it seems impossible to specify or spell out the role of Sir Syed in shaping and producing the newspaper.

Early Persian newspapers hardly made use of news items but *Zubdatul Akhbar* published news stories on its front page, which were reproduced in another newspaper, *Asadul Akhbar,* Agra. It is clear that the newspaper got its cue from *Syedul Akhbar*, which published news stories and also from other material borrowed from the reprinted English newspapers. Sir Syed was responsible for picking up news stories from English newspapers, which he also did for the *Aligarh Institute Gazette*.

Further, *Zubdatul Akhbar*'s deep interest in publishing reports on scientific discoveries and experiments indicates Sir Syed's involvement. Since the files of *Zubdatul Akhbar* are no longer available, nothing can be said authentically about the nature of Sir Syed's stint with the newspaper. Nevertheless, Sir Syed's disclosure makes it clear that he did work for *Zubdatul Akhbar,* for a while.

(c) *Loyal Mahomedans of India*:

Sir Syed had worked for two newspapers – *Syedul Akhbar* and *Zubdatul Akhbar*, before starting his first bilingual periodical, *Loyal Mahomedans of India,* which was erroneously described either as a pamphlet or as a book. Its three issues appeared within a span of two years, at an interval of a little over six months.

A close look at the three issues of *Loyal Mahomedans of India* makes it clear that it was a bilingual journal, as all three issues published material on various themes: the description of those Muslims who supported the British, the Islamic concept of Jihad and the treaty signed during the time of the holy Prophet; however, it carried the same title, *Loyal Mahomedans of India*. Had it been a pamphlet or a book, it would have carried different titles for separate topics. Further, pamphlets and books are usually not published without the name of the author.

Explaining the purpose of *Loyal Mahomedans of India*, Graham says that it was started to remind the British of invaluable services rendered to them, by the Muslims, during the cataclysmic events of 1857. Graham says:

> During and for long after the mutiny, the Mahomedans were under a cloud. To them, were attributed all horrors and calamities of that time and this prejudice was to a very great extent unjust and was regretted and resented by the Mahomedans at large. No one being apparently willing to take up cudgels in their defense, Syed Ahmed threw himself into the breach and did all in his power to rehabilitate their reputation.
>
> (Graham, 1885)

Graham certainly has a point, as the Muslims were subjected to unprecedented atrocities. Their deplorable plight prompted Sir Syed to protest against the terrible onslaught. He took up his pen to undertake the daunting task of salvaging the lives of Muslims who were writhing under the reign of repression which had been unleashed by the conquering British. He did so in order to remove the wrong impression of the rulers that the Muslims played a pivotal role in the rebellion as they considered it their religious duty to wage a war on the British. Sir Syed wrote a book titled *The Causes of Indian Revolt*.

Despite his voluminous book, Sir Syed realised that the misconception about the Muslims still persisted; hence he decided to publish a bilingual journal – *Loyal Mahomedans of India* from Moradabad. He wanted to acquaint the Government with the fact that the Muslims, in several cities, whole heartedly supported the

British in their hour of crisis. They even put their lives in jeopardy to save the British, from the rebels.

According to Hali, Sir Syed wanted to write a lengthy book on the subject in Urdu and English, to be published in parts in India and Britain, but it did not materialise.

As a result, when *Loyal Mahomedans of India* was launched, it became a bilingual journal aimed at highlighting the Muslims' loyalty to the British. It also carried the certificates, recommendations and other letters issued by the officials of the Government to the Muslims, for their unflinching loyalty. The description was also followed by the full description of the remunerations and awards received by them.

Sir Syed wanted to get it published in Urdu and English simultaneously but many difficulties came his way, which Hali enumerates:

> At that time translation from Urdu into English was an expensive business and the cost of type printing was higher than the traditional lithographic process. Hence, Sir Syed proposed that each one whose name was to be included should have borne the cost of printing of the section concerning himself. It is pity that very few people showed any enthusiasm for the project and the result was that only three installments (273 pages in all) were finally issued. These appeared from 1860 to 1861.
>
> (1979)

The first issue of *Loyal Mahomedans of India* appeared in 1860 from Moradabad. Its size was 18 × 22/8 and each page was divided into two equal columns. Each column has a width of 2 inches and a length of 6 inches. The total printed area on a page was 12 inches. Sir Syed chose a movable type instead of popular calligraphy and the Urdu text and its English translation appeared on the same page; the front page carried the name of the journal, both in Urdu and English. The English title, in bold type, occupied 75% space of the front page; its Urdu title, *Risala Khair Khuwahan-e-Musalmanan-e-Hind* (Loyal Mahomedans of India) is displayed in small type. The first issue (Part-I) is composed in gothic type. The name of the editor or the author is conspicuous by its absence. The print line, published in English, says: 'Printed by J.A. Gibson at the Mofussilite Press, Meerut, 1860.' (Title page 1 & 2 of *Loyal Mahomedans of India*, 1860)

The first issue begins with the narration of the services rendered by Sir Syed himself during the turbulent period of 1857. In order to lend credence to the description of the unprecedented and unflinching loyalty shown by the Muslims, Sir Syed refers to his own example. The narration begins with a truism:

> It is an incontrovertible truth that in the revolutions of time a general calamity arises some times of a nature so mightily overwhelming that man is completely prostrated and unhinged thereby and rendered utterly helpless in his extremity. As it were a powerful weight upon his soul tearing it down into the gulf of despair, for, at that season of crushing trial, neither virtue nor learning, nor skill nor talent, is of any avail. His nature is thoroughly changed in the estimation of his fellowmen; none has a good opinion of him, and nothing that he does claim from others any respect. Assuredly when a man is guilty of a really culpable act, there can be no extenuation for that; but when he is enveloped by the somber mantle of misfortune, even his good deeds are obnoxious to suspicion and misconstruction are either condemned in toto, or said to be found in every class and creed.
>
> (*Loyal Mahomedans of India*, 1, p. 3)

The maxim is extended too far and the introduction seems to be tedious and sluggish. The opening sentence runs into more than forty words, both in Urdu and English. It highlights the deplorable plight of socially and economically ruined Muslims. Here, Sir Syed seems to be at the best of his penmanship:

> The advice of this axiom is equally true so far as much as those men who are not under the influence of the blighting shadow of misfortune succeeded in maintaining a fair reputation; and notwithstanding that their hands may be sullied by crime yet they escape reprobation. Now the reason of dire extremity which I allude to, is that befell the Mahomedans in 1857-58. There was no atrocity committed then of which the blame was not imputed to Mahomedans although the parties really guilty may be Ramadeen and Matadeen.
>
> (*Loyal Mahomedans of India*, 1, p. 3)

Also Sir Syed ponders over the reasons that created the crisis. Turning the table on those who propagated the rumours that the Muslims wanted to overthrow the British rule, Sir Syed asserts:

> Some of the acts of horrible drama have already been exposed, but as day by day all the particulars are gradually brought to light when the naked truth stands revealed - then will this glorious fact stand out in prominent relief and become known to the universe that if in Hindustan there was one class of people above another, who from the principles of their religion, from habits and associations and from kindred disposition, were fast bound with the Christians in their dead hour of trial and danger in the bonds of amity and friendship, those people were the Mahomedans and they alone. This will actually silence the tongue of stander so loud in their condemnation.
>
> (*Loyal Mahomedans of India*, 1, p. 4)

Sir Syed's assertion, despite its polemical and rhetorical expression, looks unerring as he cited various instances which are supplemented with the letters of the British officials. He cogently argued that the rebellion was not predominantly a Muslim uprising.

In line with it, the Judicial Commissioner of Oudh, Sir George Campbell (1824–1892) termed the rebellion truly Indian in nature, as both the Muslims and the Hindus joined it with equal vehemence. It was not the Muslims alone who waged a war against the British, as Campbell refers to the Mopala Muslims of South India and Farizi Muslims of Bengal who did not join the rebellion. (Campbell, 1983, Appendix 2, p. 399)

Campbell's views were also endorsed by Surendra Nath Sen (1977) who produced a long list of Muslim rulers. He mentioned the name of the Nizam of Hyderabad and the Muslim rulers of Rampur, Karnal, Moradabad, and Dhaka. They stood by the British in their hour of crisis. Many prominent Muslims such as Qazi Ramzan Ali, Syed Ahmad Khan, Maula Baksh and Shah Kabeeruddin were the close associates of the British. (Sen, 1977)

The history of the rebellion makes it clear that the Muslims did take part in it but they did not spearhead it in the Oudh, Bihar and Central Provinces. Those who revolted against the British to topple the government were mostly Hindus. The Muslims did join them as they were those who lost their empire to the British. A number of prominent rebels who led a fierce battle against the British were Jhansi Ki Rani, Tantiya Tope and Nana Saheb and they were all non-Muslims. This aside, a number of historical evidences also endorse Sir Syed.

There is no denying the fact that the Muslims in some areas, especially in Rohilkhand and the Western part of North India, led the rebellion and Sir Syed had no justifications for them. He hardly made an effort to get them absolved of the charge of rebellion. Sir Syed writes:

> I am no advocate of those Mahomedans who joined the rebellion, on the contrary I hold their conduct in utter abhorrence as being in the highest degree criminal and wholly inexcusable – Such unworthy Mahomedans have well deserved the righteous indignation of all right thinking people but at the same time I must deprecate that wholesome denunciation against the entire class of Mahomedans.
>
> (*Loyal Mahomedans of India, 1,* 1860, p. 6 and 10)

Sir Syed was appalled by the frequency of newspaper reports that freely represented the Muslims as being everything that was vile, treacherous and contemptible. In order to thwart such attempts, Sir Syed highlighted the cases of loyalty shown by the Muslims, more especially by those in the service of the Government. Sir Syed found it pertinent to refer to his own example to stem the rot. The beginning of narration reveals a measure of modesty:

> It was not originally my intention to say concerning myself, since it did not seem to me that my humble services had been of sufficient importance to merit the gracious notice of the Government, which has done so great things for me as to surpass immeasurably my expectations. Indeed, I blush to compare my sense of unworthiness with the magnitude of the favours and considerations with which I have been honoured. Upon more mature reflection it has however seemed desirable that the author of his work should certainly make mention of certain particulars affecting himself personally, to enable the public to judge from his antecedents, his position, his character and his conduct during the rebellion. What amount of credit should be conceded to his representation and to what extent he proved himself, in the hour of peril, to be a faithful and zealous adherent of the Government he served.
>
> (*Loyal Mahomedans of India, 1,* 1860, p. 25)

Having jotted down such introductory lines, Sir Syed went on narrating his family background and his employment with the Government. He briefly mentioned the book he had written and then gave a graphic and matter of fact account of the dreadful events of 1857. At that point of time, Sir Syed held the office of Sudder Ameen at Bijnore. During the violent uprising, he decided to stand by the Government, no matter what came in his way. Sensing the imminent threat, Sir Syed decided to remain with Mr. A. Shakespeare, Magistrate, all through and for that, he forsook his residence. He did not put off from his person, the weapons with which he had armed himself.

Whatever Sir Syed had said is authenticated by the letters and certificates issued by the British officials. Mr. Alexander Shakespeare's lengthy letter supplements the narration:

> All the three officials, on whom I am reporting, have shown conspicuous loyalty but if I were required to draw a distinction, I should do so a favour to Syed Ahmed Khan whose clear sound judgment and rare uprightness and zeal could scarcely be surpassed. I feel assured his official character is so well established the independent of his official services during this crisis, his promotion to a Principal Sudder Ameen might be looked upon as certain and I trust he may soon obtain his promotion but in addition to this I recommend that in appreciation of his peculiar claims to reward, as having been mainly instrumental in securing the escape of the whole of the Bijnore party of Europeans and of his subsequent services when the district was made over to him.
>
> (*Loyal Mahomedans of India*, 1, 1860, p. 40)

The letter also mentions Sir Syed's losses at Delhi, where his property was ransacked as the rebels came to know that he was a loyal subject of the British. His loss at Delhi and Bijnore was estimated at rupees thirty thousand.

Sir Syed's exemplary courage and devotion to his official duties was acknowledged by the Government and subsequently he was promoted to the rank of Principal, Sudder Ameen. He was also provided with a pension of rupees two hundred per mensem, for his own life and the life of his eldest son. Further, a robe of honour (Khilat), comprising five pieces of cloth, three gems and a donation of rupees one thousand were also awarded to him.

The first issue of *Loyal Mahomedans of India* carried the official correspondence verbatim that makes the text quite tardy. The whole episode concerning Sir Syed is spread over thirty five pages.

Sir Syed narrates the unprecedented courage of an officer, Zuqueera Khan, posted at Jehanabad, Piliphit District, who laid down his life, while defending the British officials. Zuqueera Khan, a native of Rampur, held the office of Peshkar at the time of outbreak of violence. Sir Syed writes about him:

> He displayed zealous loyalty and performed many good services by attaching himself to the Magistrate's person, and was present at his house at all hours. When the revolt gained strength and the residence of the Magistrate's wife and children at that station was held to be fraught with peril, he escorted them in safety to Nayneetal. Having been joined by several other Mahomedans who were his friends at Nayneetal, Zuqueera Khan made himself very useful and was presented at the engagement of Churpoora and Sooltangunge in February 1858, conducting himself with indomitable gallantry. On the reoccupation of Pilibhit, he was promoted to the Tehsildar, but it was alas! Only a short lived dignity for he was soon slain by a rebel and thus perished for his loyalty.
>
> (*Loyal Mahomedans of India, 1,* 1860, p. 63)

Later, the Government gave him land and a robe of honour (Khilat) was also awarded to him. His description is also supplemented with a detailed report of Mr. C.P. Carmichael, Magistrate, and Pilibhit. Zuqueera Khan's tale is spread over 5 pages in the first volume of *Loyal Mahomedans of India.*

The subsequent pages of the first volume narrated the tales of gallantry of Abdul Khan, Kotwal, Pilibhit, Alee Mohamed Khan, soldier, Safooullah Khan, soldier, Ullay Yar Khan, soldier and Mohammad Khan, soldier. Also, an extract from the list of persons eminent for loyalty in Pilibhit was published.

The first issue also carried a fairly detailed account of Moonshi Mohamed Hussain, Serishtdar, Dewani Court, Moradabad, who had shown exemplary courage when the prisoners broke open the jail. The certificates of J. Wilson, Commander on Special Duty, Moradabad and John Wilson, Judge, are a testament to his unmatched courage.

The pages of *Loyal Mahomedans of India* are not exclusively meant for highlighting the gallantry and exemplary courage of the Muslims serving the Government but are also braced for elaborating invaluable services rendered by the Muslim landlords and nawabs. The last ten pages highlight the bravery of Sheikh Shurfooduin, a resident of Shekhpoora, Badaun District. Here, the introduction is written in ornate language:

> It would be a hopeless task to attempt a delineation of his mental sufferings to portray his load of anxiety for the safety of his precious charge amidst the surroundings or to exhibit with adequate force the ingenuity and courageous firmness with which he baffled the design of the enemy and finally triumphed over the difficulties. These things surpass the power of description.
>
> (*Loyal Mahomedans of India, 1,* 1860, pp. 64–65)

The troops revolted on May 31, 1857 at Bareilly and on the next day the troops stationed at Badaun mutinied and the soldiers abandoned their allegiance. Soon the district administration caved in; Mr. W. Edwards, Magistrate and Collector of the district, was left with no choice but to seek the help of Sheikh Shurfooduin. *Loyal Mahomedans of India* explains:

> Mr. Edward, Magistrate and Collector of Badaun, dispatched a Mahomedan sawar (soldier) to Shekhpoora to summon Sheikh Shurfoodin for his assistance. This worthy man at once responded to the call and hastily arming his relatives, friends and retainers and with some 200 men in all, he proceeded to Badaun. There, meanwhile anarchy had made fearful strides, for the prisoners had been set free, the mutineers were in possession of the Government treasure, and plunder prevailed at every side, while the air was rent with the firing of musketry. Through the scenes of fire and outrage, the Sheikh made his way to the Magistrate's house and taking him under his protection together with three other European gentlemen viz Mr. Donald, indigo planter, his son and his friend at his own house in Shekhpoora, and kept them there. Thence, he afterwards conducted them all in safety to another village of the name Kurkora.
>
> Soon the rebel troops carrying guns, 500 cavalry and an entire regiment of infantry reached the Badaun. Then the European wished to go to Puttealee, a nearby town, where the English force was posted. Sheikh escorted them across the Ganges.
>
> (*Loyal Mahomedans of India, 1,* 1860, p. 4)

Here the letters and certificates appreciating Shurfoodin's gallantry issued by Mr. A. M. Phillips, Joint Magistrate, Etah, Mr. W. Edwards, Judge, Mr. C.P. Carmichael, Officiating Magistrate, Mr. W. J. Brambly, Magistrate and Collector of Aligarh, Mr. Elliot Colvin and Mr. R. Alexandra, Commissioner Rohilcund Division lend credence to the description.

The first volume ran into eighty two pages, in which a number of specific instances were quoted where the Muslims alone protected the British. The detailed description calls attention to invaluable services rendered by the Muslims during the period of unprecedented peril. The gallantry shown by the Muslims justifies the claim of Sir Syed that one finds at the beginning of the first volume:

> It is the Mahomedans alone who stood as staunch and unshaken friends of the Government amidst that fearful tornado that divested the country, and shook the empire to its centre, and who were ready heart and hand to render their aid to the utmost extremity or cheerfully to perish in the attempt, regardless of home and kindred of life and its enjoyment.
>
> (*Loyal Mahomedans of India, 1,* 1860, p. 3)

Sir Syed alluded to a plethora of specific instances for refuting the view held by the British that the Muslims were convinced that the Christian rule in India was about to be over, as the prophecy of Shah Naimatullah clearly suggested it. Sir Syed quoted religious decrees to explain how the Muslims were enjoined by the precepts of Islam to live together with the Christians peacefully as they also believed in the prophets and held sacred, the word of God.

The second issue of *Loyal Mahomedans of India* denoted a slight but significant change. Now the name of Sir Syed, Sudder Ameen of Moradabad appeared on the title page but there was no change in print line. As discussed earlier, the first issue of *Loyal Mahomedans of India* chronicled the services of the Mahomedans who stood by the British, but the second issue proffered a perceptive and analytical discussion on the Islamic concept of Jihad (Holy War). It started with a customary prayer that every devout Muslim says when he begins something. The opening lines seemed quite appropriate in that the whole issue was devoted to a religious debate.

At the outset, Sir Syed made it clear that after having published a detailed account of several Mahomedans, who, by their good conduct and devotion had obtained appreciation and reward, he intended to chronicle the eminent services of the loyal Mahomedans. Further, he wanted to explain the true Islamic concept of Jihad which was diametrically opposed to the term 'Jihad' propagated by the mutineer and the majority of Muslims seemed to be carried away by it.

Refuting the allegation that the Muslims enjoined, by the tenets of their religion, to oppose the Christians, he pointed out:

> Whereas indeed the very reverse of this is the fact, Mahomedans admit, that there is no secret upon earth but the Christians with whom its people may maintain amity and friendship.
>
> (*Loyal Mahomedans of India*, 2, 1861, p. 95)

He quoted the Quranic prohibitions frequently to prove that the Christians were the most inclined to entertaining friendships with the true believers. He also referred to Islamic history and reminded the Muslims of an incident pertaining to the time of the Prophet when the idolatrous people of Mecca began to harass the faithful and the prophet ordered his followers to migrate to the Christian state of Abyssinia (Ethiopia).

Quoting the holy Quran and alluding to several incidents, Sir Syed tried to drive the point home that amity and goodwill always existed between the Muslims and the Christians. During the time of rebellion, a rumour gained currency that Shah Naimutullah's prophecy was said to have foretold the dissolution of the Christian empire. Sir Syed describes it as completely absurd, as Islam, per se, abominates prophecies. For Islam, no man has the divine attribute to foretell the future; hence no importance is to be attached to the prediction. Sir Syed gave a point by point rebuttal in the terse prose:

> God forbids that the Mahomedans should attach an iota of faith to the prophecies. On the contrary, it is held by us to be a grievous sin to ascribe to any mortal man, the divine attribute of knowledge of future – or to place the slightest confidence in the predictions of astrologers or indulge in the superstitions, observances of auspicious times and seasons. This being the case, how could any sensible man

> give credence to the fantasies of some unknown individual who may have chosen to amuse the credulous of a past age by playing the Prophet.
>
> (*Loyal Mahomedans of India*, 2, 1861, p. 105)

His long essay on Jihad is followed by the description of many Muslims who lend a helping hand to the British in their hour of peril.

The second volume of *Loyal Mahomedans of India* provides a detailed description of Monshi Imamuddin, Tehsildar of Moradabad, Nawab Nabee Baksh Khan Bhadoor, Delhi and Sheikh Khairuddin Ahmad Khan Bhadoor, Deputy Magistrate, Ghazipur. Sheikh Khairuddin's efforts are profusely applauded as he had kept a tight vigil on the troops posted at Ghazipur. Due to his relentless efforts, Ghazipur had not fallen to the rebels. The official reports say that Sheikh's expostulations and persuasion went a long way in allaying the suspicion of the 65th Regiment and it was kept in check.

Unlike the first issue, the narration here was divided into small paragraphs and the sentences (both in Urdu and its translation into English) were short and crisp. The prose was completely devoid of verbosity, obscure words and hackneyed phrases.

In this issue too, the narration was authenticated by many official documents and letters. It ran into eighty nine pages and it also contained an appendix spreading over ten pages. It proffered a thought-provoking discussion on Jihad for which Sir Syed sought the help of one of his learned friends who suggested that some other equally important texts, previously unnoticed, should also be referred to. The second issue also appeared in the same year (1860).

The third volume of *Loyal Mahomedans of India* was published in 1861, at the Mofussilite Press, Meerut. Now Robinson became the publisher instead of J.A. Gibbon.

The third volume too is devoted to a central theme. As we are aware, Sir Syed strove to build up a warm rapport with the Christians and he left no stone unturned to fulfil his objective. Friendship between Muslims and Christians was very close to his heart as it was a must for the speedy uplift and development of his community which was erroneously inclined to engage in confrontations with the British.

Sir Syed was an avid reader of history, metaphysics, theology and Islamic history. The sweep of his reading was amazing and he also read a particular book authored by a Christian, Lancelot Addison. The author quoted a treaty signed between the Muslims and the Christians, in the time of the Prophet. It was an old text, written in 1697.

Sir Syed reproduces the treaty verbatim on the pages of *Loyal Mahomedans of India*. He wrote the following stand first before reproducing the treaty:

> I have lately been perusing an old book by Mr. Lancelot Addison in which I found the copy of a league and covenant which in a former era, had been concluded between the Mahomedans and the possessor of Christianity. I, here give this curious document and shall be glad if any of my readers will let me know, whether in the course of their own study of Arabic History, they have seen any mention made of this league.
>
> (*Loyal Mahomedans of India*, 3, 1862, p. 178)

The above mentioned treaty, signed by the Prophet himself, had hardly come in for a detailed analysis as its text was not available. A copy of the treaty was found in the Monastery on Mount Carmel and it was sent to the King's Library in France. The treaty provides equal rights to Christians and Muslims and one can hardly find any iota of religious discrimination in the ideal Islamic society, setup by the Prophet. It stipulates:

> If any Christian commits a crime or fault, it shall be the part of the Muslimin to assist him, intercede; and give caution for him and compound for his miscarriage; liberty shall also be given him to redeem his life. Nor shall he be forsaken, nor destitute of help, because of Divine Covenant which is with them; that they should enjoy what the Muslimin enjoy, and suffer what they suffer.
>
> According to this covenant which is by the Christian just request, for confirmation of its authority, you are aligned to protect them from all calamities, and perform all offices of good will toward them, so that the Muslimin may be sharers with them in prosperity and adversity.

> Moreover, all come ought to be made that no violence be offended to them as the matters relating to marriages Viz that they should not compel the parents to match their daughters with the Muslimin; nor shall they be molested for refusal either to give a bridegroom or a bride for this act is wholly voluntary depending on their free will and pleasure.
>
> (*Loyal Mahomedans of India, 3*, 1862, p. 183)

The treaty contains many provisions that ensure the Christians and other religious minorities, equal rights. The Prophet directed the Muslims to follow it, for otherwise they would be treated as the enemies of God. It was clearly prepared to usher in a new era of goodwill and mutual trust between the Muslims and the Christians.

The Treaty that lay in oblivion for years, speaks volumes about the tolerance, generosity and benevolence of the Prophet, during the prime of Muslim glory. At the end of the documents, Abu Bakr, Omar Bin Alcherab, Osman bin Affawan and Ali Bin Abu Talib signed as witnesses. It was signed on the first day of the moon of the fourth month, the fourth year of Hegira in Medina.

The publication of the treaty went a long way in convincing the Muslims to shun their pronounced hostility towards the Christians. The excerpts of the treaty are spread over ten pages.

Similar to the previous issues, the third volume also calls attention to the gallantry shown by six loyal Mahomedans - Sheikh Tajudeen, Daroga, Moradabad, Syed Turab Ali, Deputy Collector, Bijnore, Sheikh Ameer Ali, Tehsildar, Peelibhit, Sheikh Badaruddin, Tehsildar, Auanla, Barriely, Monshi Abdul Ghani, Supplier, Railways and Mahomed Ibrahim Khan, Tehsildar, Shamlee. Seventy eight pages are devoted to their description.

If all three volumes are sifted at once, one can easily conclude that Sir Syed was the first Urdu journalist who sowed the seeds of development in journalism as he tried to instil a sense of belonging, with the Government of the day, among his readers. The first prerequisite of developmental journalism is to create a sense of belonging and Sir Syed quite successfully achieved it.

He wanted to extricate the Muslims from their medieval ways and also establish a good rapport with the British. For that, he used journalism as a vehicle. His pen was entirely directed towards alleviating the condition of Indians, especially the Muslims. At places, his prose seems to be highly emotive and persuasive. A dispassionate description, with a fair amount of objectivity, runs through all the pages of *Loyal Mahomedans of India*.

Hali points out that the three issues of *Loyal Mahomedans of India* carry a detailed account of some 18 people, many of whom had been killed by the rebels and goes on to enumerate a list of their family members. (1979: 68)

Contrary to this, the three issues of *Loyal Mahomedans of India* actually carry the description of 21 people – 18 Government officials, 2 nawabs and one supplier of railways. The government officials, mostly junior ones, two deputy collectors, Sayid Turab Ali and Sheikh Khairuddin, four Tehsildars-Munshi Imamuddin, Mahomed Ibrahim Khan, Sheikh Ameer Ali and Sheikh Badaruddin are chosen and their tales of gallantry and exemplary courage are narrated. One principal Sudder Ameen - Sir Syed himself and one Serishtdar Moonshi Mohamed Hussain also got attention.

Hali again inaccurately mentions that all three issues contained two seventy three pages but actually there are a total of two seventy seven.

At that time (1860), the cost of printing by type was very high; Sir Syed requested that the cost of the printing be borne by the persons who wanted to get their description published in *Loyal Mahomedans of India*. The proposal did not evoke a positive response; hence *Loyal Mahomedans of India* could not survive after the third volume.

References

Ahsanul Akhbar. Jan 2, 1846. Bombay.

Barns, Margarita (1940) *Indian Press*. London: George Allen and Unwin Ltd.

Campbell, George (1983) *Memories of the Indian Career.* Appendix 2. Edinburg: William Blackwood.

Graham G.F.I (1885) *Life and Works of Syed Ahmad Khan* Edinburgh and London: William Blackwood & Sons.

Hali, Altaf Hussain (1979). *Hayat-e-Javed.* Trans. K. H. Qadri and David J. Mathews. Delhi: Idara Adabiyat-e-Urdu.

Krishnamurthy, Nadig (1966) *Indian Journalism. Mysore:* University of Mysore.

Loyal Mahomedans of India (1860, 1861, 1862)

Masood, Tahir (2002) *Urdu Sahafat Uneesvi Sadi Mein.* Karachi: Fazli & Sons.

Natrajan, J (1955) *History of Indian Journalism.* New Delhi: Publications Division. Ministry of Information and Broadcasting, Government of India.

Sabri, Imdad (1955) *Urdu Sahafat Ki Tareekh,* 1.

Sen, Surendra Nath (1977) *Eighteen Fifty Seven.* Delhi: Publication Division, Govt. of India.

Siddiqui, Ateeq Ahmad (1980). *Hindustani Akhbar Navesi Company ke Ahad Mein.* Karachi: Indus Publication. Reprint.

Siddiqui, Mohammad Ateeq (1957) *Hindustani Akhbar Naveesi, Company Ke Ahed Mein.* Aligarh: Anjuman-e-Tarraqi Urdu.

Siddiqui, Mohammad Ateeq (1966) *Sooba Shumali Maghribi Ke Akhbarat wa Matbooat,* Aligarh: Anjuman-e-Tarraqi, Urdu.

The Aligarh Insitute Gazette, 12 November 1878.

10. Pioneering the First Urdu Book on Journalism

The First Vernacular Book on the Art of Journalism

Seldom does a historical fallacy that becomes omnipresent, unwittingly give way to a well-documented and a painstaking research finding. This is the reason that a majority of scholars, who are turning their attention to the history of Indian journalism, still give credit to the Punjab University, Lahore, for launching the first course in journalism as early as in 1941, under the stewardship of Professor Prithivipal Singh. The course was later shifted to Delhi and then to Chandigarh.

Contrary to the widely held view, Professor Nadig Krishnamurthy, in his authentic work on *Indian Journalism: Origin, Growth and Development of Indian Journalism from Asoka to Nehru,* points out that it was the National University at Adyar (Madras) that first started a full-fledged course in journalism. The course was started because Dr. Annie Besant was deeply interested in imparting professional training to those who wanted to be journalists and the students who joined the course got hands-on training at the office of the New India. (Krishnamurthy, 1966)

Next, it was the turn of the Aligarh Muslim University to introduce journalism as a specialised branch of academic discipline at its campus. According to Krishnamurthy, the Aligarh Muslim University offered a diploma course in Journalism in 1938 (Krishnamurthy, 1966: 174). Sir Shah Mohammad Suleiman, a judge of the Federal Court, who took over as the Vice-Chancellor of AMU, made it a point to start a diploma course in Journalism and appointed a veteran journalist, Chowdary Reham Ali Hashmi, who had considerable experience of editing both English and Urdu newspapers. Hashmi had worked with *The Leader, The Independent* and a host of Urdu newspapers. The students used to get practical training at the University press and they were also periodically taken to various newspaper offices.

The diploma course was taught in English and it was a runaway success but the untimely departure of the vice-chancellor, Sir Shah Suleiman, the ardent patron of the course, took its toll on the smooth running of the course. The dons of the University, who were sore at the introduction of this course, as they did not consider journalism an academic discipline, forced the course-in-charge to resign. The course ended abruptly and the teacher again went back to his old profession.

Though the diploma course in journalism at Aligarh was short lived, it attracted serious attention of the academic and professional world. One of the few eminent professional journalists, who took up teaching of journalism earlier in the twentieth century, Chowdary Reham Ali Hashmi made path-breaking advancements in journalism education when he wrote the first book in Urdu, on the art of journalism, *Fann-e-Sahafat*. It is perhaps the first book in any Indian language, on the theoretical framework and epistemological foundations of the profession. It was written at a time when people believed that journalists, like poets, were born and not made.

His book *Fann-e-Sahafat*, written in 1938, was published by the premier Urdu organisation, Anjuman-Tarraqi Urdu in 1943. The book, a first of its kind in any Indian language, comprises of three sections and twenty seven chapters. It runs into two twenty seven pages and has illustrations and photographs of printing machines. It is replete with a number of professional exercises, as Hashmi was of the view that journalism meant being and doing, not theorising (Hashmi, 1938). The book made people realise that journalism was not to be taken as a casual activity or a pastime but a profession, that called for a flair for writing, creativity and a deep understanding of the human nature. It required professional competence and sound theoretical knowledge. Journalism was to be more akin to law, medicine, engineering and other such academic disciplines that required extensive professional orientation.

The first section of the book, consisting of fifteen chapters, deals with the definition, scope and purpose of journalism. A brief history of journalism and the then present scenario of newspapers also comes in for detailed discussion. The author rightly points out that the newspaper had rapidly become the lifeline of modern living as it provided much-needed information and knowledge on a range of subjects. Superstitions and other social evils could only be wiped out with the help of newspapers, as they unfailingly spread education and awareness. Explaining the prospects of journalism as a career, Hashmi spells out the duties and responsibilities of an editor, assistant editor, news editor, sub editor and reporter. By joining the profession, one could get instant fame but one could not be assured of a decent salary; in fact, the author goes on to explain candidly that at that point of time, journalism was a mission with very little monetary benefits.

The fourth chapter of the first section begins with the definition of a newspaper. The author ropes in some eminent journalists such as Adolph Mayor to make his point. He concludes:

> The newspaper is a commercial venture that is heavily dependent on selling news and reasoned opinion. The whole business is shaped by the editorial, advertisement and circulation departments and these sections are all equally responsible for ensuring the success of a newspaper.
>
> (Hashmi, 1938: 13)

The author analyses various definitions of news and makes a candid distinction between events and news. For him, an event could only become news if it had the potentiality to evoke human interest. The term, 'human interest' usually lies in unusual events that conjure up emotions, interesting details of human life, money matters, religion, personalities, sports, politics and government affairs. Notwithstanding some apparent pitfalls, the list sums up eloquently, what makes news. Novelty, proximity, timeliness and prominence are vital elements of news. Hashmi's categorisation of news is quite perceptive as he does not restrict it to geographical boundaries. One has to remember that news is usually divided by geographical terms.

The author proffers a discerning discussion on the art of writing for newspapers and periodicals. For him, the frequent use of conversational words and short and declarative sentences, paves the way for smooth reading and a journalist is supposed to write in an easy-to-understand style. Cliché-ridden language, antiquated expressions and trite metaphors must not find their way into the writing. The journalist must learn the art of brevity, and verbosity should be kept at bay. The chapter also provides some important tips on how to write effectively. Explaining the structure of editorials, Hashmi concludes that the editorial invariably has three parts: present state of affairs, arguments and conclusion; and the editorial, more often than not, closely resemble some sort of exhortation or a wise advice.

The author exhorts 'cubs' ie. apprentices and amateur journalists to make it a point to write daily and that even if they fail to get the nod of the editor, they should not lose heart. He narrates an anecdote from when he was with *The Independent*. The editor had asked him to write a piece daily but without the guarantee of its publication. He wrote for four months continuously and then one day, some of his lines appeared in the newspaper. It filled him with immense pleasure. His advice to budding journalists is to maintain a high degree of equanimity that usually paves the way for success.

With an even-handed attention to flair for writing and common sense, he explains the professional duties and responsibilities of the reporter, sub editor, news editor, assistant editor and editor. He rightly describes the sub editor as the 'Unsung Hero' who takes the pains in brushing up the text and making it error free, but he hardly gets recognition from any quarters. The author also focusses on headline writing and explains the point system, which, with the advent of Video Display Terminal (VDT) has become redundant, but some other concepts such as the page makeup, a vital aspect of newspaper production, that was assigned to sub-editors, escapes his attention. At that time, the copy editor designed the page but now the layout is usually done by the layout or the art editor.

Since the book was basically written for Urdu newspapers, a separate chapter is devoted to the art of translation. He quotes the blunders in translation that marred the Urdu newspapers. One newspaper translated 'Benghazi captured (a city of Libya) recaptured' into Urdu as '*Ben Ghazi Phir Pakar Liya Gaya*' or the English idiom, "It rained cats and dogs" as '*Kutton aur Billiyon Ki Barish Haui*'. A growing acquaintance with both languages is a must for a translator, who is known as a sub-editor in Urdu newspapers, the author rightly concludes.

Having explained the duties and responsibilities of editorial staff, the author turns his attention to other vital aspects of the profession. According to him, an interview is the bedrock of journalism and a reporter must know how to get along with different kinds of people. He has to be good at persuasion so that he can obtain the required information from the person being interviewed, without losing any time.

Hashmi puts a premium on objectivity and fairness in news writing and firmly believes that a news report should never take the shape of polemics. The journalistic writing undoubtedly draws its sustenance from rhetoric and persuasion but views are to be supported by documentary evidence. A journalist must not be carried away by hearsay, sentimentalism or prejudice. Snap judgments have virtually no role in news writing.

The article is the most effective vehicle of expression and one is supposed to shun his detached outlook and can take sides if he wishes to. Arguments related to both sides are to be placed in the proper perspective, however.

He spells out various forms of reviews: book review, film review, music review, art review and the like and asserts that review writing is a specialised genre that needs more than news sense or common sense. Any person with a way with words cannot become a good reviewer unless he develops a keen insight into the art form. A familiarity with the literary theories is also required. The reviewer must be gifted with aesthetic sensibility.

The second section, comprising chapters on proof reading, printing, composing room, machine room, photo printing, and binding, is aimed at providing vital information on various aspects of newspaper production. The practical exercise of proof reading lends credibility to the book. Litho printing has come in for detailed discussion. Two photographs of a litho printing machine and a double feeder machine are also included. The methods of composing Lino, Mono and Intertype are also explained. In this section, technical terms are frequently used and this makes for heavy reading.

The third section of five chapters bears fruits of the painstaking efforts. There are separate chapters on the administration, advertisement, circulation and printing departments. Proper emphasis is placed on highlighting the importance of circulation. Not much is written on advertising and one wishes to see more on copy writing and kinds of advertisements in the book. The last chapter harps on proper and harmonious coordination among various departments. They have to work as an organic whole if success is to be achieved.

Some minor blemishes apart, *Fann-e-Sahafat*, the first book on the art of journalism in any Indian language, is clearly braced for acquainting readers with the theoretical and practical aspects of journalism.

References

Hashmi, Chaudhary Reham Ali (1938) *Fann-e-Sahafat*, Aligarh: Anjuman-e-Tarraqi Urdu.

Krishnamurthy, Nadig (1966) *Indian Journalism: Origin, Growth and Development of Indian Journalism from Asoka to Nehru*. Mysore: University of Mysore.

11. The Contribution of Urdu Journalists to the First War of Independence

India's awe-inspiring evolution from a fragmented, nascent and peripheral country to an invincible world power owes much to its inhabitants, who, notwithstanding their different religious, ethnic, linguistic and geographical affiliations, espoused the cause of nation building. Much ink has been spent over the invaluable contribution of different religious, social and linguistic groups and also the political parties who put up a fight against subjugation and exploitation but the stupendous contribution of the Urdu speaking people, especially Urdu journalists, has hardly been made the object of in-depth analysis. This chapter is aimed at supplementing what has been ignored deliberately or unwittingly, since long.

Seldom does the Muslim-dominated, protest-prone Urdu press awake one's memories of the sterling role that it played during India's first war of independence. The contemporary Urdu press, the third largest numerically, has largely been perceived as a body of casual writing that borders on the highly sentimental 'kitsch'. The debatable nature of such a widely-held view could only be deflated, if the role of the Urdu press, during the eventful period of the freedom struggle, is made the object of a close study. It looks pertinent to turn one's attention to Urdu journalists who wielded their pens to rouse feelings against the alien rule, as a result of which the British took severe punitive measures against them.

Contrary to the well established and dominant English newspapers of the nineteenth century, such as *The Englishman, The Friend of India*, *Bengal Harkaru*, *Delhi Gazette* and *Bombay Times* that invariably described the first attempt to overthrow the British as 'Mutiny, 'Rebellion', 'Sedition', 'Sepoy Revolt', 'Insurgency' and 'Uprising', the nascent Urdu press had provided much-needed stimulation to the armed struggle by describing it as 'The first War of Independence', a 'Popular Uprising', a 'Freedom Movement', a 'People's Movement' and a 'Natural Revolt against Subjugation'. The Urdu newspapers, published from all parts of the country, extended wholehearted support to those who made an attempt to raise their voice against the oppressive rule by publishing news reports, editorials and articles in favour of the armed struggle launched by Indians.

Urdu journalism of the nineteenth century holds the unmatched distinction of producing the first journalist who laid down his life for engendering patriotic feelings by exposing the misdeeds of the deceitful alien rule, which unleashed an unprecedented reign of terror on the helpless Indians. The journalist, Moulvi Mohammad Baqar, Editor, *Delhi Urdu Akhbar*, faced death at the hands of a firing squad, as soon as the British conquered Delhi (20 September 1857). It is shocking to note that the protagonist of freedom, who happened to be the editor of a widely circulated Urdu daily, was put to death without a formal trial. He became the first martyred journalist of India.

Moulvi Baqar's supreme sacrifice aside, a number of Urdu newspapers such as *Sadiqul Akhbar* (Delhi), *Tilism-e-Lucknow*, *Seher-e-Samri* (Lucknow), *Kohinoor* (Lahore), *Akhbar Murtazai* (Peshawar), *Desi Akhbar* (Multan), *Habibul Akhbar* (Badaun), *Umdatul Akhbar* (Bareilly) and the like, made all efforts to bolster the torchbearers of the freedom movement. Devoting almost all the space to highlighting the valour of Indian soldiers who took on the mighty British army, the newspapers urged people to extend their unflinching and constant support to the armed struggle. Urdu newspapers published hard-hitting editorials, articles, news reports and verses, aimed at raising passions against the foreign dispensation.

The first Urdu newspaper of North India, *Delhi Urdu Akhbar* was brought out by Moulvi Mohammad Baqar, in February 1837, from Delhi (Khan, 1991). It was a weekly, printed on four pages of 12 X 8 inches, published every Saturday. Its issues of 1857, available at the National Archives, Delhi, unfailingly highlight the social and cultural milieu and political life of Delhi, where a complete decline and degeneration had set in. It carried a plethora of news items related to international events, the affairs of Native States, the Royal Court and the East India Company. Further, the activities of a helpless ruler, confined to the four walls of the castle, are narrated in a permanent column, *Huzoor-e-wala* (His Excellency).

The range of news coverage was extremely wide and the newspaper was rightly regarded as a complete newspaper, fully compatible with its English contemporaries. It appointed correspondents at various cities of the country, to obtain the latest news. Moulvi Mohammad Baqar had put premium on authenticity and objectivity and asked the correspondents not to make use of hearsay and unattributed information and rumours. *Delhi Urdu Akhbar* was always held in great esteem by both Indians and the British, though its circulation hardly ever crossed the three digit mark.

Delhi Urdu Akhbar, through its selective publication of news reports, articles, and editorials, instigated its readers against the British rule and when Indian soldiers stormed Delhi on May 11, 1857, it devoted its entire front page to highlight their unprecedented gallantry. *Delhi Urdu Akhbar*, known for its restraint, had given up its detached point of view and showed little sympathy for the victims of the Indian soldiers' violence. The issue of May 17, 1857 carried a detailed first hand report of the incomparable violence that erupted in Delhi. It was perhaps the first example of 'spot reporting' (ie. directly reporting from the place where an important event occurred) in Urdu journalism.

The report, written in first person narrative, instead of the usual third person, says:

> The present scribe too came out of his house to see things for himself, inspired as he was by a regard for the glory of his Faith and hearing the sound of gunfire. I was confronted by a strange sight: people

> were running from Kashmiri Gate side into the market. Personal safety was no doubt in danger, but dearer to me than my personal safety was the desire for unusual sights and the other equally strong desire to give a faithful eye-witness account of events to my readers. As I moved forward, I heard gunshots at a place a little ahead of me. Soon, I saw the Sahib Bhadur running away for his life, sword in hand and a native following him with gun, close at heel. In the rear was a crowd of common people some with sticks in their hands, others with bamboos, chasing the beleaguered Englishmen at hot speed. They hunted down from Zeenat Bara towards the canal.
>
> (*Delhi Urdu Akhbar*, May 17, 1857)

Moulvi Mohammad Baqar was an avowed enemy of those who were loyal to the British and he would come down heavily upon them. According to him, their support to the alien rule essentially betrayed their own faith and it also made it clear that they hardly cared for their motherland:

> It has often been heard that quite a large number of Hindus and Muslims are still loyal to the Christians and have thus betrayed their own faith. Such traitors are the well-wishers of the British and wish to see them victorious. They give them vital information secretly. It is obligatory on the part of all Muslims and Hindus to beware of them, to learn about their activities and to bring them to book so that others might learn from their example.
>
> (*Delhi Urdu Akhbar*, May 24, 1857; quoted in *A History of Urdu Journalism*, p. 97)

Delhi Urdu Akhbar never shied away from joining the issue with the English newspapers who always supported the British, and when Indians got the better of the Englishmen, it published an editorial of refutation:

> Where have gone *the Englishman* and the *Friend of India* – and their unflinching and unequivocal support to awe-inspiring administration and discernment of the British? Make them see how the poverty-stricken, impecunious and indiscreet Indians from cities and villages have ripped the edifice of their empire to nothing.
>
> (*Delhi Urdu Akhbar*, May 24, 1857; quoted in *A History of Urdu Journalism*, p. 97)

In order to thwart the victory march of the freedom fighters, the East India Company tried to create a rift among Indians on religious grounds and it circulated a proclamation which described the rebellion as the handiwork of Hindus. It urged the Muslims to get themselves dissociated from the rebellion as they were men of faith and shared a lot in common, with the Christians. They were not supposed to be overwhelmed by infidels. The British announced a number of steps including general clemency and release of attached properties to assuage the feelings of the beleaguered Muslims. Moulvi Baqar warned his co-religionists not to believe the British.

In a cogently argued editorial on the rebellion, Moulvi Baqar raised a pertinent legal question. He stated that if the Indian soldiers revolted against the company, the company should have approached the emperor. Who had given the British the right to wage war against the emperor?

With a view to arresting the attention of the compatriots and also to keep their morale high, *Delhi Urdu Akhbar* changed its name. The issue of July 12, 1857 carried a new title – *Akhbar ul Zafar*. The new name, *Zafar,*means 'victory' and it was also the pen name of the emperor – Bhadur Shah. The newspaper mentioned that the new title was suggested by the emperor himself. The newspaper started appearing on Sundays instead of Saturdays, in defiance of the Christian decree that stipulates no newspaper be issued on Sunday.

This aside, *Delhi Urdu Akhbar* published a poem by Mohammad Hussain Azad, son of Moulvi Baqar, who was also a famous poet, stylist and scholar of Urdu, Persian and Arabic. The poem vividly portrayed the gradual but decisive decline of the British at the beginning of the armed struggle. It also reflected the popular sentiments aroused by the first war of independence. It begins with an incisive comment:

> It was only yesterday that the Christians
>
> Were the championed ones and the world providers
>
> But today all their prudence melted away
>
> And their conquering army proved ineffective

(*Delhi Urdu Akhbar*, May 24, 1857)

The euphoria of the freedom struggle drew its sustenance from the pen of Moulvi Baqar who was eliminated as soon as the Company gained control over the situation. Some historians have erroneously linked the execution of Moulvi Baqar to the killing of Mr. Taylor, the principal of the Delhi College. They alleged that the famous journalist first gave shelter to Taylor and later handed him over to the rebels. This is not true, as Moulvi Baqar published the first hand account of the dance of death in Delhi, in his newspaper. The spot report did mention the killing of Mr. Taylor. The report gives a first-hand account:

> ... I was soon overwhelmed by a sound of such magnitude that I had thought to be the Doomsday trumpet. I soon realized that the magazine had been blown away. A cloud of dust covered the atmosphere; huge stones and pieces of masonry were blown apart like birds and leaves of trees in a dust storm. Later, it was learnt that a few of the Holy Victors had climbed the wall of the magazine in order to kill Englishmen, their wives and children, who had enclosed themselves within the building for safety. Those imprisoned within did their best to defend themselves, even fired a couple of shots but in vain. In the confusion, however, following the blowing up of the underground tunnel, some of those surrounded did manage to escape but perished later. It is heard that Mr. Taylor, the Principal of the College, was among those surrounded inside the magazine. His days were not perhaps numbered, so he lived on to die the next day in the vicinity of the same police station. His dead body remained naked and covered with blood lying on the ground throughout the day. Spectators said he then truly looked like a dervish-beggar with a face laden with dust. (Khan, 1991)

The account of the killing of Mr. Taylor conclusively proves that Moulvi Baqar was in no way connected with it. Had he been involved in it, he would have certainly mentioned it in his report, as his editorials showed his indomitable courage to take on the British.

An arrest warrant was also issued against his son Mohammad Hussain Azad, who published a revolutionary poem in the newspaper. Mohammad Hussain Azad fled to Sonepat but his family was thrown out of Delhi.

Another Urdu newspaper published from Delhi, *Sadiqul Akhbar*, played a pivotal role in moulding public opinion against the foreign rule. The newspaper was launched by Syed Jameeluddin Khan 'Hijer' in July 1854 (Khan, 1991). He championed the cause of freedom struggle and wrote extensively to expose the misdeeds of the East India Company. The importance of *Sadiqul Akhbar* could be gauged from the fact that the public prosecutor referred to it frequently during the trial of Bhadur Shah Zafar. Syed Jameeluddin harped on patriotic and nationalistic feelings in his editorials.

Jameeluddin Khan 'Hijer' urged the Indians, especially the Muslims, to wage a holy war against the oppressive government and he hoped that Iran would extend support to the Indian freedom struggle as it was also against the British. In its issue of 6 July 1857 *Sadiqul Akhbar* published a religious decree, signed by thirty five Islamic scholars who described the armed struggle as 'Jihad' (Holy War). It published a number of editorials, articles and news stories aimed at highlighting the gallantry of freedom fighters. As soon as the struggle subsided, the company arrested Jameeluddin Khan. He was sentenced to jail for three years.

Public Prosecutor, Major F.G. Hornet, in his long statement, tried to prove that the mutiny of 1857 owed much to a conspiracy plotted by the Urdu press, in collaboration with the Royal Court. Jameeluddin Khan served a sentence for three years but the imprisonment did not put a brake on his journalistic zeal. Having been released from jail, he launched another newspaper, *Lawrence Gazette*, from Meerut in 1864. (Masood, 2002)

The annexation of Oudh led to widespread discontent against the British rule and many newspapers launched a vociferous campaign for the restoration of Oudh. Moulvi Mohammad Yakoob Ansari launched a weekly, *Tilism-e-Lucknow*, on 25 July 1856. It appeared every Friday and it exploded the myth that Wajid Ali Shah's rule was bogged down by complete administrative disorder. A marked disenchantment with the British rule could be glimpsed through the pages of the *Tilism-e-Lucknow*:

> Since the day the English began to rule this city, the mischief mongers have come into ascendancy. There is deceit and mischief

> everywhere. Suits were filed against the Mahals and Begums in civil and criminal court. (Khan, 1991)

Tilism-e-Lucknow vehemently denounced the so-called constructive reforms launched by the Company and it described the steps as repressive and coercive, aimed at gaining ascendancy over the native population, by roping in deceitful and dubious methods. It published a number of editorials and articles when the armed struggle for freedom began. It persuaded people to wage a religious war against the alien rule and tried to boost the morale of the oppressed people of Oudh. A news report appeared in the newspaper, saying:

> Someone has again lighted the flame of rioting and violence (at Lucknow); the Mandyvan cantonment was set on fire; the puzzle has not been solved. Strange are the tricks played by fortune? It is said the (the trouble began) since the day the new type of cartridges arrived. These cartridges arrived. These cartridges led to rioting in cantonments of Achanak, Ambla and Ferozepur. These riots caused discomfort to many and deprived others of their jobs. Such rioting seems to have started here in our native city too. Everywhere people are talking about what happened recently. (Khan, 1991)

With the outbreak of violence against the British, the paper discontinued its publication. Its last issue appeared on 8 May 1857.

Umdatul Akhbar (Bareilly) stood firmly behind Fateh Bhadur Khan who took up arms against the Company. By following in the footsteps of *Delhi Urdu Akhbar,* it also changed its title. It became *Fatehul Akhbar* which served as an organ of the freedom fighters. When Bareilly was recaptured, the company ordered the closure of this newspaper and its press was subsequently impounded. (Khan, 1991)

Habibul Akhbar (Badaun) wrote extensively in support of the First war of Independence and as a result, its editor was sent to jail and the press was removed for breaking the law. (*Aligarh Institute Gazette,* March 19, 1875)

Akhbar Murtazai (Peshawar) also extended whole-hearted support to the freedom struggle and its editor was arrested on the charge of publishing provocative and seditious material. (Sabri, 1952)

Since the files of early Urdu newspapers have become extinct, one cannot make an objective assessment of the contribution of Urdu journalism to India's first War of independence but some issues of the above-mentioned Urdu newspapers, preserved at the National Archives and Aligarh Muslim University, did throw light on the invaluable contribution of Urdu journalism. The revolutionary character of Urdu newspapers prompted the British public prosecutor to accuse Urdu newspapers of persuading people to fight against the British.

In 1866, Sir Syed launched his famous multilingual weekly, *The Aligarh Institute Gazette* and four years later, he started *Tahzibul Akhlaq*.

Not infrequently, Sir Syed has been fallaciously stigmatised by many as a sycophant of the British rule. There is no denying the fact that Sir Syed sometimes praised the British rule extravagantly but he also did write with pugnacity, against British officials who subjected their Indian subordinates to cruelty and barbarity.

Sir Syed, through his writings, made it clear that self respect was the most venerated and invaluable possession. He never compromised on this count and whenever an attempt was made to tarnish the image of Indians, the *Aligarh Institute Gazette* was quick to protest. It tried to thwart the attempts of some haughty British officers who unleashed a reign of terror. As a sequel to the first war of independence, some ruthless and cruel British officers took pride in physically assaulting the low-ranked Indian employees. Their fiendish and inhuman attitude resulted in the merciless killings of many Indian employees.

In 1875, a Peshawar based British official thrashed an Indian waiter to death; the *Aligarh Institute Gazette* published a well-argued denunciatory article. Sir Syed found it appropriate to publish a highly censorious article, as the self respect of Indians was in jeopardy. He also deplored the attempt of the English newspapers to justify the killings:

> In Peshawar, Lieutenant Garrison Saheb Bhadur has inflicted a lethal blow to an Indian waiter and as a result that poor fellow died

> instantly. Curiously, the doctors declared that prolonged illness had made him weak and led to his death. The English newspapers reporting the incident pointed out that the officer pushed him lightly but he died. The light blow used by the English journalists, clearly indicate their dishonesty.
>
> (*Aligarh Institute Gazette*, April 23, 1875)

The author referred to many such instances and asserted this was a testament to the fact that the blood of an Indian was considered inferior even to the water used for cleaning the guns of Sahibs. He regretted that whenever the British officials killed an Indian, a fit of provocation was always cited as the justification of their acts.

Sir Syed points out that when an Englishman got assassinated, the English newspapers would publish the tales of brutality of the Indians and the stories of mercifulness and generosity of the Sahib would start appearing. For him, their attitude was in no way compatible with the announcement of the Queen, who invoked the principle of impartiality by describing her white and black subjects as her two eyes and also that no one was entitled to get preference over the other.

Sir Syed hardly minced words in asserting that he did not recall any instance where an oppressed Indian got justice enough to suffice the Indians. Deeply regretting judicial discrimination, he calls attention to the fact that no Englishman was hanged for killing an Indian; on the other hand, however, if a Britisher's dog got killed at the hands of an Indian, a hefty fine and at least a one-year imprisonment was imposed on the Indian. Provocation was always cited as the cause of attack and the Indian invariably charged with disobedience and malice. He raised a pertinent question by asking the Queen whether she sent her countrymen out to protect and impose the law or to put their lives into futher misery and hardships.

The above-mentioned article was no exception; whenever an attempt was made to besmirch the self-respect of Indians, the *Gazette* unfailingly published penetrating articles.

The Government of the N.W. Province took offence at the publication of such an article and issued a warning to the *Gazette*. The official memo no. 69999, dated April 20, 1875 was subsequently issued:

> Undersigned is directed to invite the attention of the editor of the *Aligarh Institute Gazette* to the impropriety and injustice of the criticism hazard at page no. 181 and 182 of the issue of the 19th March 1875, and to remind him that the paper is taken by the government for distribution among schools but that Government cannot be expected to subscribe to any paper which expresses opinion as those in the article in question.

The intimidating tone of the letter did not deter Sir Syed from continuing the berating and reproving campaign against the arrogant and self-conceited British officials. How can a person who published such spiteful articles be described as an apologist for the British rule? The warning also absolves the *Aligarh Institute Gazette* from heaping fulsome praise on the British rule in India. Since no serious attempt was made to turn attention to such articles, Sir Syed is still branded as an ally of the British.

References

Aligarh Institute Gazette. March 19 and April 23, 1875.

Delhi Urdu Akhbar, May 17, 24, 31, 1857.

Khan, Nadir Ali (1991) *A History of Urdu Journalism (1822–1857)*. New Delhi: Idrah-i adabiyat-i Delli.

Masood, Tahir (2002) *Urdu Sahafat Uneesvi Sadi Mein*. Karachi.

Sabri, Imdad (1952) *Rooh-e-Sahafat*. Delhi.

Trevelyan, G.O (1864). *The Competition Wallah*. London and Cambridge: Macmillan and Co.

12. Abul Kalam Azad's Journalistic Conquests

Journalism, since its inception, has been perceived as the most effective agent of social activation, and no other social and intellectual activity can vie with journalism in propelling forward the process of social change. This is the reason that a number of political leaders, educationists, social reformists and ideologues of the pre-independence era such as Raja Ram Mohan Roy, Sir Syed Ahmad Khan, Pandit Madan Mohan Malviya, Lala Lajpat Rai, Mahatma Gandhi, Maulana Mohammad Ali and Zafar Ali Khan had started their periodicals, not for literary excellence or for carving out a niche for themselves in the power structure, but for moulding public opinion against the foreign rule. There is no denying the fact that their efforts bore fruits but their missionary zeal and rhetorical and polemical writings were not fully compatible with the epistemological and professional framework of journalism.

Much has been written about Maulana Abul Kalam Azad's political statesmanship, unrivalled erudition and unequal intellectual eloquence in proffering a perceptive and innovative discussion on the topics having definite bearing on the metaphysical and physical aspects of life.

His journalistic excellence, the hallmark of his creative genius, has also come in for detailed debate. It has been pointed out, time and again, that Azad's lucid but verbose prose style unfailingly charted a new path in Urdu journalism.

Maulana Azad started his career as a journalist early, at the age of 11 years, when he published *Guldasta*. Before launching his famous journal, *Alhilal*, he had tried his hands at various reputed periodicals including *Al Misbah, Ahsanul Akhbar, Khadange-Nazar, Lisanul Sidq, Al Nadwa, Wakeel, Darul Saltanat* and the like. This chapter is aimed at placing Azad's journalistic endeavours in professional perspective.

No other famous journalist, political leader, educationalist or litterateur can compete with Azad, as far as adequate acquaintance with the professional framework of journalism, is concerned. Azad's illustrious intellectual career drew its sustenance from journalism and at a very tender age, he realised the importance of journalism and envisaged his role as a journalist. Azad writes:

> Now I have been feeling more inclined towards this new nourishment than poetry and believed the biggest thing a man could achieve, is to write articles that appear in newspapers with his name. The next and the most important step is to become an editor of a newspaper or journal.
>
> (Malihabadi, 1958)

Journalism, as the most effective mode of expression, had fired Azad's imagination at an early age and prompted him to get himself fully acquainted with its professional aspects and Azad's growing familiarity with the profession is manifested in his article, 'The Art of Journalism' that appeared in the *Makhzan*, May, 1902. The article discusses the historical background of the profession, the definition of news, the kinds of newspapers, the benefits of newspapers and the opinions of the eminent persons about newspapers.

At the outset, Azad points out, quite rightly, that the unprecedented and fast development of Europe and America owed much to newspapers. In those countries, everybody read newspapers and were, thus, well-versed in almost every topic. For him, the newspaper was nothing but a guiding light that persuaded people to give up bad habits and prompted them to adopt the rational world view that would pave the way for all round progress. Man, by his very nature, is wayward and he desperately needs a mentor. The newspapers catered exactly to this need and they were the best guides that prompted people to tread the path of progress, by making them fully aware of all possible dangers which may have come their way.

Concluding the article, Azad cited the examples of famous Governor Generals of India, such as Sir William Muir, Sir Alfred Loyal, Sir Griffin, Sir Richard Temple Garth and some others who took up journalism after their retirement. Their journalistic articles are still held in high esteem. This bears testimony to the fact that journalism is a wonderful and interesting profession that attracts a number of known and established scholars. (Azad, 1902)

Perhaps it was the first detailed and authentic article in Urdu, that covered some vital aspects of journalism, notwithstanding its historical aspects and some other pitfalls and fallacies. Azad was deeply concerned with the theoretical and empirical aspects of the profession and strove to get himself acquainted with the latest trends of the discipline.

For him, the process of national development could not be propelled forward unless the most powerful medium of moulding public opinion – Journalism – was roped in. In 1904, he wrote a note in *Lisanul Sidq,* under the heading – 'Interesting information about newspapers' in which he paid tribute to Japan for achieving tremendous success in all walks of life that prompted Europe to describe it as the 'Britain of Asia'. The march to progress, indeed, owed much to the growth of newspapers, as in 1880, there was only one newspaper in Japan but in 1904, there were more than 600 periodicals. These periodicals were on par with the periodicals of the west. (Azad, 1904) [My translation]

For Azad, journalism was certainly more than a casual activity that strove to bring about social change. With even-handed attention to subject matter and presentation, Azad formulated a model of journalism and opened new vistas in Urdu journalism. If Azad's writings that appeared in the *Lisanul Sidq, Alhilal* and *The Albalagh* are sifted at once, the salient features of his model would become clear.

Before Azad, the purpose of journalism was not clearly spelt out in Urdu; verbosity, subjectivity and polemics were the hallmark of his journalism. Sir Syed's writings were the sole exception. Azad, for the first time in Urdu, tried to fulfil the three purposes of journalism – to inform, to educate and to entertain, simultaneously. Azad's popularity grew enormously with the publication of *Alhilal* in 1912. Azad basically tried his hands at weekly journalism. Earlier, no distinction had been made between weekly and daily journalism. The term 'journalism' used to refer to newspapers, journals, and other periodicals. Further, views and news were not considered separate entities.

At subject matter level, Maulana Azad placed premium on enlightenment. He was an avowed enemy of narrow-mindedness and the ideal of Hindu-Muslim unity was very close to his heart. He did not make any compromise on this issue and waged a relentless battle against communalism. He made it a point to prove that journalism is not only a form of necessarily ephemeral writings but is also an effective medium for initiating a dialogue with people, on all questions of their lives. Through his writings, he tried to educate people collectively.

The cardinal principle that runs through all his writings is to propagate righteousness and curb thrift and depravity. His writings underscored that point unfailingly. Azad's editorials and articles were directed towards alleviating the conditions of people, especially the Indian Muslims. He opposed the two-nation theory vehemently, though the majority of Indian Muslims were swayed by the rhetoric of the Muslim League. The subject matter of Maulana Azad's journalistic writings is discussed time and again but the parameters of his journalism, are hardly ever elaborated.

Maulana Azad was the first Urdu journalist who made a distinction between newspapers and journals. In his article on 'Journals', published in *Alhilal,* dated 20 July 1912, Azad wrote that newspapers can be put into two broad categories: the dailies that are common and the journals that usually appear weekly or fortnightly. They carry more profound, focussed, explanatory and analytical articles to expand the mental horizon of the readers.

> It lies midway between newspapers and monthlies and presents a judicious mix of the political discourse of dailies and scholarly articles of monthlies. But the journal does not find it appropriate to

> publish news received by the wire and reports on current affairs, sent by correspondents, as one finds in dailies. The journal assumes that its readers are aware of daily news and political issues; it publishes an edited version of important parts in the form of a debate.
>
> (*Alhilal*, 4 August 1921) [My translation]

Clearly, Maulana Azad has a pertinent point in the distinction between journals and dailies and his political journal *Alhilal* revolved around it. It did carry a number of news stories related to the war between Turkey and Britain, but as Maulana pointed out, they were published, not as news stories, but as brief summaries and the editor also raised relevant questions about the war.

Having been completely dissatisfied with the nascent journalism in Urdu, Azad made it a point to supplement what had been completely ignored. Enrichment was his basic concern and he published seminal and thought-provoking articles that were intended to enlighten people on all possible questions related to their life. The media has been pursuing the 'Infotainment' model. If one had to define Maulana's model of journalism, he would describe it as the 'Inforichment' model that revolved around a definite purpose. In order to provide the much needed solace, guidance and to arrest the feeling of inertia, Maulana launched *Alhilal*. For him, unvarnished information hardly had any importance, as it must be placed in a perspective so that it may stir the sense of belonging.

Alhilal's persuasive prose was consistent with his view of journalism as being the purveyor of truth. It is made up of an evocative idiom that is lifted to a higher moral tone. His style is replete with long drawn and obscure words, but it clearly has a rhythm that is both invigorating and harmonious. Azad frequently employed humour and satire to drive home the need for social and political reforms. His weekly extended an invitation to thinkers to win a worthy audience for their scholarly writings. Azad always held accuracy and fairness in high esteem and never relied on hearsay information. *Alhilal* used to publish translations of news from famous Arabic and English newspapers namely *Alminar, Almureed, The London Times, The Manchester Guardian* etc.

In addition to selecting the subject matter carefully, that unfailingly corresponds to his "Inforichment model" and missionary zeal, Azad took pains in modelling *Alhilal* according to the pattern of the Western periodicals. For him, journalism was not just confined to writing articles and editorials but was also related to page makeup, display, use of type, publication of photographs and cartoons and the ethics of publishing advertisements. No other periodical, prior to the publication of *Alhilal* touched upon these vital professional aspects of newspaper production.

Maulana Azad always vouched for freedom of the press; whenever an attempt was made to throttle the press, Azad left no stone unturned for preserving the freedom of the press. On Azad's intent, the Indian Press Association came into being, to safeguard the interests of the vernacular press. He never shied away from having a dig at the British government, which initiated punitive action against a number of vernacular newspapers.

The sweep of articles published in *Alhilal* is amazing and Azad was the first journalist who exposed his readers to a plethora of topics that go beyond ephemeral events. *Alhilal* has many firsts to its credit and reveals Azad's journalistic dexterity. Azad gave equal importance to the display of newspapers, though early Urdu newspapers virtually had no idea of page make-up. Azad increased the size of printed area and *Alhilal* published on pages of size 20×30/4 and each page was equally divided into two columns. Usually it had 16 pages, excluding four title pages.

The front page carried the masthead of *Alhilal* and 2/5 space was devoted to the nameplate. The front page always had a double or single column photo and content table and the details of photographs used to appear on the front page. In order to facilitate reading, Azad started publishing the details of the content and photographs as no other Urdu newspaper, ahead of *Alhilal* carried this information on the front page.

Azad always felt a strong aversion to the poor display quality of Urdu newspapers. For him, calligraphy was the main hurdle that afflicted the printing process. He points out that a calligrapher, quick at his task, four stones and a hand press were all that one required for starting an Urdu newspaper. In order to make the newspaper visually attractive, Azad turned his attention on 'type' and he imported type from Turkey, for the purpose. He incorporated important changes in the width and mould of the existing type, before placing the order abroad.

Alhilal was the first Urdu weekly that used quite legible and attractive type and it started a new trend in Urdu printing.

The circulation of *Alhilal* had reached 10,000 copies per week, an unprecedented circulation figure, which proved that type could gain currency in Urdu, despite apparent detestation. The use of attractive and distinctly legible type gave a palpable look to *Alhilal*. The pages were equally divided into two columns, and the words on a given line were almost the same and it gave the pages a harmonious look.

The display of a newspaper is basically shaped by visual material – photographs, graphics, illustrations, maps and charts. Before the advent of *Alhilal*, photographs were hardly used by Urdu periodicals. The lack of photographs would give a clumsy look to the newspapers. *Alhilal* has many firsts to its credit – the frequent use of photographs is one of them. Azad made special arrangements to obtain action photographs of the war and always published photographs of prominent Muslim thinkers and scholars. He made it a point to publish at least 4 to 6 single and double column photographs in every issue of *Alhilal*. The photographs published in *Alhilal* were quite distinct and clear, as Maulana used the half tone technique in making the blocks of the photographs. He writes in this regard:

> We bought a new machine for printing half tone and we also publish photographs separately. Further, we got a double crown machine for the purpose. We will start publishing colour photographs soon and the ink we use is of the best quality. (*Alhilal*, 13 July 1913)

Azad's intent on the use of photographs makes it clear that he was fully aware of the professional make-up of the newspaper page. The use of photographs lends credibility to the accompanying story and the photographs of eminent figures inspire people to emulate them.

Since Maulana Azad had a reasonable acquaintance with the professional framework of journalism, not only did he focus on content, printing technology and display principles but also set a professional code for publishing advertisements. Advertisements. are an integral part of journalism. No newspaper could survive without adequate advertising revenue. The first daily of the country, *Hickey's Gazette* (Calcutta, 1780) was more concerned with advertisements than transmission of news. Advertising is the most effective medium of raising money. Early Urdu newspapers hardly paid attention to advertisements and some of the eminent persons who launched newspapers looked down upon advertisements.

Even Sir Syed believed that the publication of advertisements infringed upon the right of readers who subscribed to newspapers for obtaining news. These sorts of views on advertising, clearly, demonstrate professional naivety.

Maulana Azad was fully aware of how advertisements could boost a newspaper. *Alhilal's* first cover of the title page carried a detailed note on advertisements that clearly manifests his professional know how. It said that the preparation of an advertisement and its publication was a full-fledged art in Europe.

The first thing about an advertisement is that it must have something that arrests the attention of people, over and above the other material of the newspapers. English newspapers and journals employ several strategies and methods for good advertising but these are not possible in stone printing. For example, an advertisement may carry an attractive halftone or engraved picture, have the material set in attractive script, may publish it in block print or prepare a chart that could contribute to the advertisements acquiring a distinct look in the newspaper. This would help increase the readership of the papers, having caught the attention of readers. These are difficult tasks in type printing.

Alhilal was the first Urdu daily that could arrange for it, but the rate of advertisements would have to be different and that could be obtained through correspondence.

This shows that Maulana was fully aware of the importance of display advertisements. How could an advertisement be made eye-catching? The above-mentioned description underscores that point.

In the issue of August 20, 1912, *Alhilal* carried a full-page advertisement that laid down the conditions of publication of advertisements. It said that advertising rates would be charged per square inch, if the advertisement was less than half a page. If an advertisement was provided space on the inside pages, by discarding some material, it would become more visible, but for this, a twenty five percent surcharge would be levied.

Journalism was a sacred mission for Azad; hence he did not approve of advertisements that were related to immoral activities. *Alhilal* made it clear that it would not carry advertisements related to any kind of promotion of gambling, wine and related activities; also those related to medicines of venereal diseases and anything that could be against public morality.

In short, the above discussion makes it amply clear that Azad was the first journalist who propounded a model of journalism that may be known as 'Inforichment' and his journals reveal his keen professional insight.

References

Azad, Abul Kalam. 'Editorial'. *Alhilal,* August 4, 1921. Reproduced by Uttar Pradesh Urdu Academy. Lucknow, 1988.

Azad, Abul Kalam. 'Interesting Information about Newspapers'. *Lisanul Sidqi.* April 1904.

Azad, Abul Kalam (1902). 'The Art of Journalism'. *Makhzan.* Quoted in Qutubullah. Ed. *Maulana Azad Ka Nazariya Sahafat.* Lucknow: Uttar Pradesh Urdu Academy, 1988.

Malihabadi, Abdul Razzaque (1958). *Azad Ki Kahani, Azad Ki Zabani.* New Delhi: Hali Publishing House.

Index